Physical Characteristics of Cesky Terrier

(from the Fédération Cynologique International

Body: Oblong. Upper line, not straight because loins and rump are always moderately arched. Withers, not very pronounced; neck set on rather high. Back, strong, of medium length. Loins, relatively long, muscular, broad and slightly rounded.

Rump: Strongly developed, muscular; pelvis moderately slanting. Hip bones often slightly higher than the withers.

Tail: The ideal length is 18 to 20 cm; relatively strong and low set. At rest hanging downward or with a slight bend at the tip; when alert the tail is carried saber shape horizontally or higher.

Hindquarters: Hind legs strong, parallel, well angulated and muscular. Lower thigh, short. Hock joint, set relatively high, strongly developed. Hind feet, smaller than the forefeet.

Belly: Ample and slightly tucked up. Flanks well filled.

Skin: Firm, thick, without wrinkles or dewlap, pigmented.

Size: Height at withers between 25 to 32 cm. Ideal size for a dog, 29 cm; for a bitch, 27 cm. The weight must not be less than 6 kg or more than 10 kg.

Coat: Hair long, fine but firm, slightly wavy with a silky gloss. The Cesky Terrier has two varieties of coat color, gray-blue and light-coffee brown.

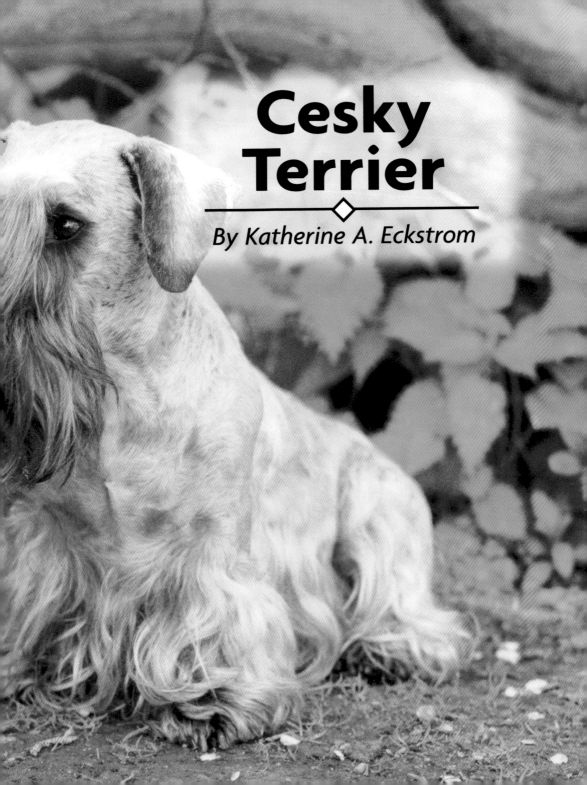

Cesky Terrier

By Katherine A. Eckstrom

Contents

KENNEL CLUB BOOKS: **CESKY TERRIER**
ISBN: 1-59378-357-4

Copyright © 2005 • Kennel Club Books, LLC
308 Main Street, Allenhurst, New Jersey, USA
Cover Design Patented: US 6,435,559 B2 • Printed in South Korea

Photography by Isabelle Francais, Gabriela Hajnová, Carol Ann Johnson and Alice van Kempen
with additional photographs by:

Paulette Braun, T.J. Calhoun, Carolina Biological Supply, Bill Jonas, Dr. Dennis Kunkel, Tam C. Nguyen, Phototake and Jean Claude Revy.

Illustrations by Patricia Peters.

The publisher would like to thank all of the owners of the dogs featured in this book, including S. Clark, A. Dreizehnter, Katherine Eckstrom, Gabriela Hajnová, Angelika Hummel, R. Kolárová, J. Kuntová, G. Merkx, John Moody, L. Nilsson, J. Paulinová, C. Richardson, A. Venema, M. Weser, Roswitha Wick and Jane Withers.

The Cesky Terrier started as a "dream" cross between a Scottie and a Sealyham, both being terrier breeds.

HISTORY OF THE

CESKY TERRIER

SMALL, SLIM AND ELEGANT
It all began with a dream. Frantisek Horak, noted top-ranking geneticist and cynologist with the Academy of Sciences in Czechoslovakia, had this dream...a dream of a terrier that was small, slim and elegant, a true go-to-ground open-field-working terrier.

Mr. Horak (1909–1996) was an avid hunter, Scottish Terrier breeder and all-breed FCI judge. In 1932 he purchased his first dog, a Scottish Terrier, having seen the breed in 1928 on the cover of the magazine *Dog*. In 1934, while working in Pilsen, he had the opportunity to work this dog in the Thurn-Taxis area, which abounds in small game, fox, badger, rabbit, wild boar and deer. This Scottie proved to be a very ardent hunter. Therefore Mr. Horak decided to breed the Scottish Terrier.

Also at this time, due to his membership in the Cynology Club in Pilsen, Mr. Horak formed a friendship with Mr. Cervenka, who bred Scotties and Sealyham Terriers. These two men shared

Scottish Terrier.

their working and breeding experiences, and thus began the dream of "something between both of these breeds (Scottie and Sealyham) which could lead to a more successful 'working result' terrier."

Every breed of dog was originally created by cross-breeding to obtain the desirable characteristics wanted in that **Sealyham Terrier.** particular breed. Once

established, a breed's "type" is maintained by breeding pure, thus the term "pure breed." In 1938, when the kennel Lovu zdar was born, Mr. Horak stated that the Cesky Terrier should be small, slim and elegant. These desirable traits are the criteria by which all Cesky Terriers have been measured and still are measured today.

In 1940, Mr. Horak moved his family and kennel to Klanovice. Unfortunately, the war years (1939–1945) and the Communist years interfered with any trial breeding. The first mating was in 1949 between Donka Lovu zdar (a Scottish Terrier bitch) to Buganier Urquelle (a Sealyham Terrier dog). The resulting litter consisted of three pups, and only one male survived. However, a careless hunter killed this dog, Adam Lovu zdar, in 1951.

In 1950 another breeding attempt took place. This time the Scottie bitch Scotch Rose was bred to the Sealyham Buganier Urquelle, resulting in a litter of six. One male, Balda Lovu zdar, met the requirements of Mr. Horak's vision: drop ears to give protection when hunting in the brush or working underground; a brindle-type coat, which ranged in color from platinum to charcoal gray; a narrower chest; and longer legs for faster movement. Balda Lovu zdar was

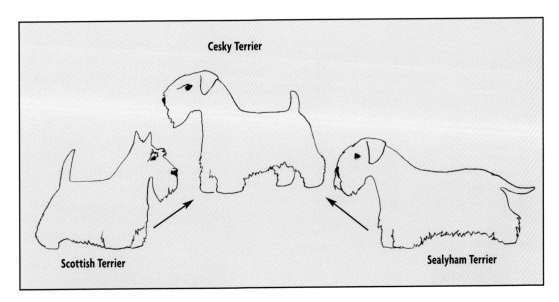

Cesky Terrier

Scottish Terrier

Sealyham Terrier

CZECH YOUR HISTORY BOOK

Czechoslovakia came into being as an independent nation upon the dissolution of the Austro-Hungarian Empire at the end of World War I. It continued as such until having most of its territory (Bohemia and Moravia) occupied by Hitler's National Socialist regime in 1939, with Slovakia being set up as a puppet state.

Having been absorbed into the Soviet Empire in 1948 (its Ruthenian territory had already been taken by the Union of Soviet Socialist Republics in 1945), what was left of Czechoslovakia became independent again in 1989, when the Soviets' socialistic empire started to implode. In 1993 it broke into two separate nations, the Czech Republic and Slovakia, and thus the two nations remain today.

later bred with his mother, Scotch Rose, and two more pups with drop ears, the dog Dareba Lovu zdar and the bitch Diana Lovu zdar, were born. These breeding attempts were reported to the Czech Terrier Club, and Mr. Horak requested this new breed be named the Cesky Terrier.

Diana Lovu zdar later became the foundation dam of the breed. She was bred with the dog Jasans Amorous Artilleryman, who was a son of Buganier Urquelle. In this litter there were two dogs and one bitch, Fantom, Furiant and Fenka (all ending in the kennel affix Lovu zdar). Fantom and his sister Fenka were bred and produced one bitch, Halali Lovu zdar, who later proved to be the pillar of the stock. Halali

Although similarities between the three breeds exist, the Cesky is a breed of its own, not just a modified version of the ancestral breeds, the Scottish and Sealyham Terriers.

and Fantom were bred, and one dog resulted. This was a brown-nosed dog, who later proved to be sterile.

It's believed that the brown color is inherited from the Sealyham, since it has never been known in the Scottish Terrier. Fantom Lovu zdar was bred with his mother, Diana Lovu zdar, and the mating produced one dog, Chytry Lovu zdar, and one brown bitch, Iris Lovu zdar. With only these few brown pups born up to and

The Cesky Terrier has reached beyond the borders of his homeland and attracted fanciers in many countries. Here is a group of Ceskies being shown in the UK.

including 1987, it was determined that the brown pigment gene must be in Fantom Lovu zdar, his mother Diana Lovu zdar and the female produced by the mating of Fantom and Halali. However, in 1994 Hana Petrusova's del Monte kennel produced Vladyka, who was brown in color, out of Kent Ahoj and Fortuna Kirke.

Although the first 15 litters were mixed, from the 16th litter on every litter has met Mr. Horak's requirements for the standard and has bred true. In 1989, due to problems of infertility and immunity, permission was given by the Fédération Cynologique Internationale (FCI), the ruling canine organization of continental Europe, for an infusion of Sealyham blood, thus creating Line 1a. Therefore, Line 1 refers to the original dogs, Line 1a to the dogs from the Sealyham

infusion and Line 1b to dogs from a questionable breeding of Dolly Vivat to Eso Lovu zdar.

THE CESKY TERRIER COMES TO THE UNITED STATES

The July 1, 1971 edition of the *New York Times* featured an article and photograph of the Cesky Terrier Javor Lovu zdar, thus introducing the breed to the US. Efforts were made to import these dogs into America but, due to the political situation in what was then Czechoslovakia, it was not possible.

NORTH AMERICAN REGISTRIES

In the US, the Cesky Terrier is registered with the Foundation Stock Service (FSS) of the American Kennel Club and is recognized by the American Rare Breed Association, the United Kennel Club and the Continental Kennel Club. In Canada, the breed enjoys full recognition by the country's major registry, the Canadian Kennel Club.

The first Ceskies to arrive in the US came from the Netherlands on June 16, 1987. One kennel sent 19, and 4 came from another Dutch kennel. In 1988 the Cesky Terrier Club of America was established, as well as a minor club. The CTCA published their first newsletter in 1989. The CTCA combined with the American Cesky Terrier Club, which combined with the National Cesky Terrier Club on January 1, 2005 to form the National Cesky Terrier Club of America, all this in preparation for the breed's entrance into the AKC.

Good Choice Hanky Panky Pecka is a representative of the breed from Sweden.

The Cesky's friendly and fun nature makes him an attractive choice for Junior Handlers.

In 1990 it became possible to import dogs directly from their homeland and thus add fresh bloodlines to the US dogs. Until this time, Ceskies had been imported from Germany, Norway, Sweden and occasionally Finland. Ceskies today are also coming from England and Canada. Statistics from 2003 show that there were approximately 500 Ceskies in the USA for that year.

CESKY TERRIERS AROUND THE WORLD

The FCI registered the Cesky Terrier as a breed in 1963. The road traveled out of the former Czechoslovakia was not easy for the Cesky Terrier. There were a

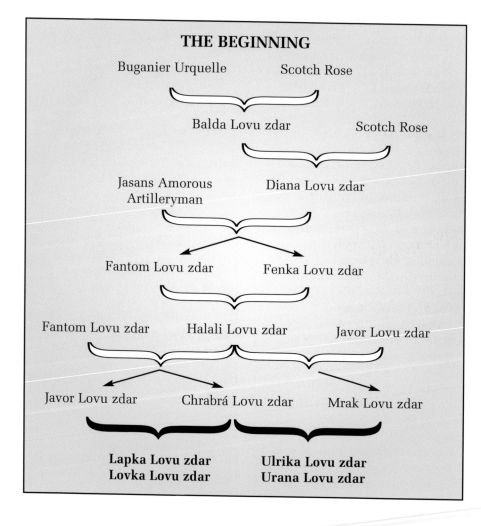

THE BEGINNING

Buganier Urquelle   Scotch Rose

Balda Lovu zdar   Scotch Rose

Jasans Amorous Artilleryman   Diana Lovu zdar

Fantom Lovu zdar   Fenka Lovu zdar

Fantom Lovu zdar   Halali Lovu zdar   Javor Lovu zdar

Javor Lovu zdar   Chrabrá Lovu zdar   Mrak Lovu zdar

Lapka Lovu zdar   **Ulrika Lovu zdar**
Lovka Lovu zdar   **Urana Lovu zdar**

The Cesky Terrier has been featured on postage stamps in Czechoslovakia along with other breeds.

few kennels at the time in the former East Germany and, as a point of interest, Javor Lovu was the first Cesky exhibited there. To Sweden's kennels, Mr. Horak traded the dog General Lovu zdar and, in whelp, Oslavia Lovu zdar for a pony. Thus began the foundation for the Cesky in Scandinavia. Mr. W. Derksen from Holland sent all of his Ceskies to Finland's Dibasa Kennel.

After the lifting of the Iron Curtain, Ceskies were given as gifts or sent as "holiday guests" to western countries. The breed is now seen in Germany, Holland, France, Belgium, Switzerland, the United Kingdom, Australia, Scandinavia, Poland, the United States and Canada. The Cesky is now recognized by all major registries around the world, except the American Kennel Club (AKC). The breed is seen at national and international shows, and Mr. Horak would be pleased with the Best in Show wins garnered by Ceskies at FCI shows.

ACKNOWLEDGMENTS

We wish to thank and acknowledge the following resources for breed references: *Cesky Terrier* by Narcisa Liskova, *Toto je Cesky Terrier* by Hana Petrusova, handouts from the Horak/Paulinova family, Fédération Cynologique Internationale (FCI) for the standard, American Cesky Terrrier Club, Friends of the Fancy.

This work is dedicated to the memory of Int. and Multi-Ch. Chlap Lovu zdar, the most titled Cesky Terrier to date, and the last dog whelped by Mr. Horak.

CHARACTERISTICS OF THE
CESKY TERRIER

PERSONABLE AND VERSATILE
Small, slim and elegant. Avid hunter, loving companion and guardian of his domain. These descriptions only begin to define the Cesky Terrier. To own a Cesky is to love a Cesky, that is for sure! Ceskies are basically sweet in temperament and not given to excessive barking; rather, their barking is mostly limited to alerting their owners. They make great house dogs, but Ceskies do not thrive in kennel environments. They crave companionship. As a hunter, the Cesky is truly an "all-arounder" who scents, hunts, goes to ground, retrieves, tracks and swims.

I wish to share the following excerpt from Barbara Barker of Vitava Kennels, with her thoughts

> **PARTY ON!**
> Ceskies are very social and love to be with their owners. They are the life of the party!

about the Cesky Terrier Calvin Bohemia USA and his antics:

"In many ways, the Cesky Terrier is an all-purpose dog. Proud Cesky owners like to point out that the Cesky, while definitely all terrier, can do the jobs of most other types of dogs as well. A good example is Calvin Bohemia USA, who, at one-and-a-half years old, is a very busy dog. He lives on a farm in the northwestern United States and performs all the traditional terrier duties. He kills rats, he hunts rabbits (although he hasn't caught one yet, he keeps them away from the vegetable garden) and he even goes to ground after

Earthdog or water dog? The multi-talented Cesky enjoys getting his paws wet just as much as he enjoys getting them dirty!

Sharing the comforts of home with a favorite young friend makes any Cesky Terrier a happy dog.

moles. But unlike some terriers, the Cesky can coexist peacefully with many other types of animal, including other dogs, cats and large livestock like horses and cattle.

"But Calvin's talents don't stop there. He is also an excellent sporting dog. He loves to flush quail out of the underbrush, which his low-slung body allows him to penetrate easily. He also, like many Ceskies, has strong retrieving instincts. In the city or suburbs, this takes the form of fetching a ball, which many Ceskies will happily do for hours.

Most Ceskies also enjoy the water and seem to be natural swimmers.

"The Cesky Terrier also exhibits some of the characteristics

CESKIES ON THE WEB
For more information, we recommend the following websites:
- www.cesky.net (National Cesky Terrier Club of America)
- www.ceskyusa.com (US)
- www.canadiancesky.ca (Canadian National Cesky Terrier Club)
- website.lineone.net/~atter (UK)
- www.volny.cz/Kchct (Czech Republic)

of the working dogs. Calvin is an excellent watchdog; he takes his job of protecting his home and his people very seriously. He likes to perch on the back of the couch, where he can see out the window, to make sure nothing sneaks up on us! And if something does, he has a loud 'big-dog' bark. However, again unlike many other terrier breeds, Ceskies do not bark excessively—only when they have a good reason. Calvin is also very protective of his owners, especially his mistress. He is wary of strangers and will not trust them until he is sure they have no bad intentions. Once he gets to know someone, however, he is friendly with them.

"In addition, Calvin is also a herding dog. He doesn't show any interest in sheep or goats, but he loves to herd chickens! We taught him early on that chickens are not prey, so he never hurts them. But he does keep them in their place. If they venture onto the lawn or the flower beds, he chases them back to the chicken yard. That is something we never taught him—he just seems to know where the chickens belong and where they don't.

"And finally, the Cesky Terrier has many of the endearing qualities of the Toy Group. Ceskies are small enough to be lap dogs, and they are also couch potatoes *par excellence.* They like nothing better than to be snuggled near their human companions. On weekend mornings, Calvin thoroughly enjoys lolling in bed between us, on his back, with his legs straight up in the air."

In conclusion, the Cesky Terrier can fit into a wide variety of living situations, as long as he is part of the family and included in activities. And he has the energy and the talent to partici-pate in just about any activity: from earthdog trials to agility competitions; from the show ring to therapy work; or just as the ideal family companion. This is truly a big dog in a small body!

INTERVIEW WITH MR. HORAK
Aside from personality traits, physical characteristics are also important to fanciers and prospective owners. Ceskies should look like Ceskies! Because of the development of the breed

and several misjudgments made at exhibitions due to unfamiliarity with the standard or misinterpretation, Mr. Horak thought it wise to publish "The Explanation of the Standard" in the magazines *Nachrichten des Klub für Terrierzuchter* and *Hund, Freund des Menschen,* both in 1985. The breed standard is explained in more detail in the following chapter of this book, but Mr. Horak's comments are worthy of inclusion here to help owners better understand correct Cesky type.

In his article, Mr. Horak writes the following: "The breed originated by crossing the Scottish and Sealyham Terriers. It has become a compromise of both breeds. The official standard of the FCI (recognized in 1963) is the foundation for the judging of the Cesky Terrier.

"The indicated shoulder height of the Cesky Terrier is 27–35 cm, although, after years of breeding practice, it seems that most animals reach 27–29 cm. Compared to the original breeds, the Cesky Terrier is higher-legged and sprightlier due to its lighter

weight (not heavier than 6–9 kg). The chest size must not be less than 45 cm and not wider than 50 cm.

"The head is not as narrow (at the top) as that of the Scottish Terrier, but at the same time not as broad as that of the Sealyham. The eyes are smaller than those of the Sealyham Terrier. The ears are clearly bent (V-shaped) above the skull and are not as big as those of the Sealyham Terrier.

"The jaw is long and powerful with a very good set of teeth. The neck is sufficiently strong and suppler than those of the two ancestral breeds.

Popping up to say hello is a curious pair representing both colors seen in the breed.

FELICIE LOVU ZDAR
The first Cesky from Mr. Horak's Lovu zdar Kennels in Klanovice, Czechoslovakia, was imported into the US by the author in 1992: Int., Mex., ARBA, NCTC Ch. Felicie Lovu zdar.

Garex Alzbeta relaxes with his Briard buddy Garex Baron.

"The front of the dog is not wide, and the chest is more round-shaped than it is deep so that there is more space between body and floor. The elbows do not protrude, but move freely alongside the body (are therefore not situated under the body). The back is not short and not long—of average length.

"The back is not so straight as that of the Fox or Welsh Terrier. Behind the loins, the back slopes slightly, but not as strongly as in the Dandie Dinmont Terrier. The hindquarters are strong, but not wide. The front of the dog is relatively straight and parallel, and very angular just as the hindquarters. There is room for free movement of the front and hindquarters.

"Apart from the hair on the legs and other parts of the body, where it acts as protection against injury, the hair is only kept long on the front of the face (beard and eyebrows). The hair on the legs, beard and underside of the body must not be too exaggerated. On the body, the coat length is 1.5 cm (required for the show ring). The hair must be slightly waved on the back.

"According to the standard, the Cesky's tail must point toward the floor when the dog is at rest, but during activity it may be slightly bent toward the front. It is certainly not considered incorrect if the end of the tail is pointing upward, but it must not be curled or otherwise held over the back.

"The standard mentions two basic colors—gray with a black nose and brown with a brown nose. From these, several variations exist—dark-gray/brown-gray, lighter brown, light-gray and light-brown. Besides the foundation color of the Cesky Terrier, yellow, optical white and gray markings are allowed (just as in animals with "black-and-tan" and "brown-and-tan" coloration).

"White markings on up to 20% of the total body surface are also allowed. These white markings are mostly on the chest, legs, underside of the body and point of the tail. A white blaze is considered undesirable. As far as quality is concerned, the animals with up to 20% white markings are considered equal to the animals that are completely pigmented (solid-colored).

"Lighter markings (yellow or gray) must not be confused with white markings. These two color variations are allowed in the Cesky Terrier, either solid gray or brown, or two colors (black-and-tan or brown-and-tan). These yellow or gray markings on mature dogs can even appear to be optical white.

"In general, it is better for the Cesky to be small and light rather

than too big and heavy. In reality, many examiners do not judge the Cesky Terrier according to the standard. Proof of this is that, at national and international exhibitions, many Cesky Terriers receive a good judgment while their chest size and proportions are considerably bigger than the standard allows.

"Only recently, examiner Mrs. Hrabakova has measured the chest of the Cesky Terrier. The judges must be aware that their judgments work like a sieve. Their decisions about what is correct and incorrect will trickle down to future generations of the breed. Through their judgments, dog-show judges play a role in the

The Cesky Terrier was originally called the Bohemian Terrier.

future development of the Cesky Terrier, or any breed for that matter."

CESKY TERRIERS IN THE ARTS

The Cesky Terrier has been an actor in films, a hero in a novel and an image pictured on postage stamps and medallions, to name a few. Orlice Lovu zdar was the model in 1965 for artist Mirko Hanak's design for a Czechoslovakian postage stamp that was issued to mark the occasion of the general meeting of the FCI.

The Cesky Lumpidus Kirke has appeared on the big screen, where he was seen hunting wild boar, and he has also appeared in the television production *Zen Stufen Zum God*. Axio Bohemius was introduced, by Mr. Horak, in the television broadcast *Klub der Jugend,* in which Mr. Horak added commentary about the breed. In 1962, Mr. Horak introduced Javor Lovu zdar on TV as well.

Batul od Stareho Jalovce became the hero of the book

Evaluating the size of the chest is an important issue in judging the Cesky Terrier.

Robin, written by Z. Frybova. Lumpidus Kirke and Carman z Libockeho Dolu were photographed for a poster that was printed for the International Exhibition of 1982 in Brunn. Lady Kirke and Besy Lovu zdar modeled for a children's coloring book by the artist Ms. Jana Rozan. In 1987, a revealing article on the breed appeared in the Swiss magazine *Hund* in which the development of the breed was described in great detail and was documented with extensive information and many photos.

TOP DOG
The most titled Cesky in the world is Multi-Ch. Chlap Lovu zdar, pictured here. He had 25 titles and 5 Bests in Show, and was owner/handled by the author, Katherine Eckstrom.

With a Cesky on each side, this owner enjoys the ultimate in canine companionship and the best of terrier personality.

CESKY TERRIER

FÉDÉRATION CYNOLOGIQUE INTERNATIONALE STANDARD FOR THE CESKY TERRIER
(Czech Terrier; Terrier Tcheque; Tschechischer Terrier; Terrier Checo)

FCI Standard No. 246
Translation: Mrs. Dipl. Ing. K. Bechová and Mrs. R. Binder-Gresly.

Date of Publication of Original Valid Standard: February 19, 1996.

Classification: Group: III (Terriers); Section: 2 (Small Sized Terriers). *Without working trial.*

Origin: Czech Republic.

Utilization: Formerly a terrier

A head study of a beautiful example of the breed from the Netherlands. The dog's expression tells volumes about the breed's intelligence and keenness.

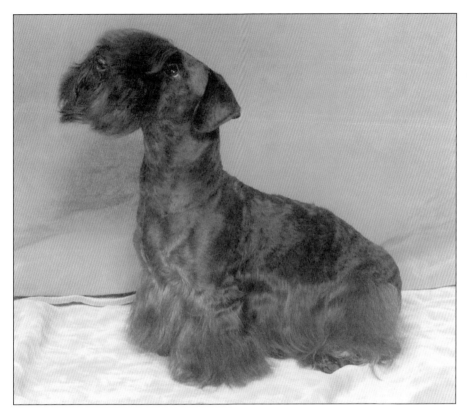

ACTC and ARBA
Champion Von
Guenzburg's
Serena's Song.

breed for hunting foxes and badgers, today more a house- and companion dog.

Brief Historical Summary: The Czech Terrier is the result of an appropriate crossbreeding between a Sealyham Terrier dog and a Scotch Terrier bitch, with the aim to develop a light, short legged, well pigmented hunting Terrier, with practical drop ears, easy to groom and easy to train. In 1949 Mr. Frantisek Horák from Klánovice near Prague started to

improve the breed by fixing their characteristics. In 1959 these dogs were shown for the first time, and the breed was finally recognized by the FCI in 1963.

General Appearance: Short legged, long haired, well made and well muscled terrier with smallish drop ears, of a rectangular format.

Temperament/Behavior: Balanced, non-aggressive, pleasant and cheerful companion, easy to train;

A Cesky in profile, correctly groomed for the show ring, demonstrating correct type, balance, substance and proportion.

Occipital protuberance easy to palpate; cheek bones moderately prominent. Frontal furrow only slightly marked.

Stop: Not accentuated but apparent.

FACIAL REGION
Nose: Dark and well developed. It should be black on terriers with a gray-blue coat and liver-colored on light-coffee brown terriers.

Nasal bridge: Straight.

Jaws/Teeth: Strong jaws. Scissors or level bite; complete dentition (the absence of the 2 M3 in the lower jaw not being penalized). Teeth strong, regularly aligned and set square to the jaw.

Lips: Relatively thick, fitting neatly.

Cheeks: Cheek bones not too prominent.

Eyes: Of medium size, slightly deep set, with a friendly expression; well covered by the overhanging eye brows. Brown or dark brown in gray-blue coated dogs, light brown in light-coffee-brown dogs. Eyelids black in gray-blue dogs, liver-color in light-coffee-brown dogs.

Ears: Of medium size, dropping in such a way as to well cover the orifice. Set on rather high and

somewhat reserved towards strangers; of calm and kind disposition.

Head: Shaped like a long, blunt, not too broad wedge, the plane of the forehead forming a distinctive breaking with the bridge of the nose.

CRANIAL REGION
Skull: Not too broad between the ears and tapering moderately towards the supraorbital ridges.

Head study of a Cesky showing proper proportion and structure as well as proper grooming for the show ring.

falling flat along the cheeks.
Shaped like a triangle, with the
shorter side of the triangle at the
fold of the ear.

Neck: Medium long, quite strong,
carried on a slant. The skin at the
throat is somewhat loose but
without forming a dewlap.

Body: Oblong.

Upper Line: Not straight because
loins and rump are always
moderately arched.

Withers: Not very pronounced;
neck set on rather high.

Back: Strong, of medium length.

Loins: Relatively long, muscular,
broad and slightly rounded.

Rump: Strongly developed,
muscular; pelvis moderately
slanting. Hip bones often slightly
higher than the withers.

Chest: More cylindrical than deep;
ribs well sprung.

Belly: Ample and slightly tucked
up. Flanks well filled.

Tail: The ideal length is 18 to 20
cm; relatively strong and low set.
At rest hanging downward or with
a slight bend at the tip; when alert
the tail is carried saber shape
horizontally or higher.

FAULTS

Thin ewe neck, dip in shoulders, short body and lack of angulation behind.

Short thin neck, loaded shoulders, toes out in front and gay tail.

LIMBS
Forequarters: The forelegs should
be straight, well boned and
parallel.

Shoulders: Muscular.

Elbows: Somewhat loose, yet
neither turned in nor out.

Forefeet: Large; well arched toes

and strong nails. Pads well developed and thick.

Hindquarters: Hind legs strong, parallel, well angulated and muscular.

Lower thigh: Short.

Hock joint: Set relatively high, strongly developed.

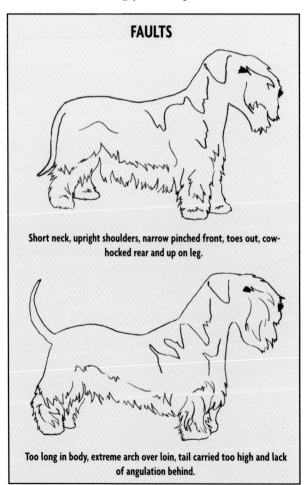

FAULTS

Short neck, upright shoulders, narrow pinched front, toes out, cowhocked rear and up on leg.

Too long in body, extreme arch over loin, tail carried too high and lack of angulation behind.

Hind feet: Smaller than the forefeet.

Skin: Firm, thick, without wrinkles or dewlap, pigmented.

Gait/Movement: Free, enduring, vigorous, with drive. Gallop rather slow but lasting. The forelegs extend in a straight forward line.

COAT
Texture: Hair long, fine but firm, slightly wavy with a silky gloss; not too much overdone. The Czech Terrier is groomed by scissors (clipping). At the forepart of the head the hair is not to be clipped thus forming brows and beard. On the lower parts of the legs, under the chest and belly the hair should not be clipped either. In show condition the hair at the upper side of the neck, on the shoulders and on the back should not be longer than 1 to 1.5 cm; it should be shorter on the sides of the body and on the tail and quite short on the ears, cheeks, at the lower side of the neck, on elbows, thighs and round the vent. The transition between clipped and unclipped areas should be pleasing for the eye and never abrupt.

Color: The Czech Terrier has two varieties of coat color:
• gray-blue (puppies are born black)

- light-coffee-brown (puppies born chocolate brown)

In both color varieties yellow, gray or white markings are permitted on the head (beard, cheeks), neck, chest, belly, the limbs and around the vent. Sometimes there is also a white collar or a white tip on the tail. The basic color, however, must always be predominant.

SIZE
Height and Weight: Height at withers between 25 to 32 cm. Ideal size for a dog, 29 cm; for a bitch, 27 cm. The weight must not be less than 6 kg or more than 10 kg.

IDEAL MEASUREMENTS
Height at Withers: males, 29 cm; females, 27 cm.

Length of Skull: males, 21 cm; females, 20 cm.

Width of Skull: males, 10 cm; females, 9 cm.

Girth of Thorax (behind elbows): males, 45 cm; females, 44 cm.

Length of Body: males, 43 cm; females, 40 cm.

FAULTS: Any departure from the foregoing points should be considered a fault and the seriousness with which the fault should be regarded should be in exact proportion to its degree.

- *Weak construction.*
- *Temporary loss of nasal pigmentation (snow nose).*
- *Weak, short or snipey foreface, with weakly developed teeth.*
- *Absence of one (1) incisor, canine hold back.*

Apolenka Orest Kalimera, an outstanding Cesky.

The beautiful XiXa Kvitko.

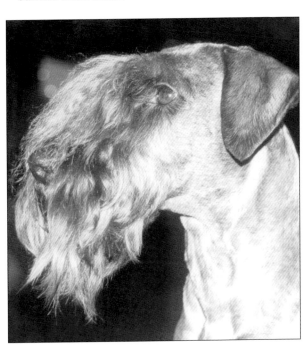

IDEAL MEASUREMENTS		
	Dog	**Bitch**
Height of withers	29 cm	27 cm
Length of head	21 cm	20 cm
Width of skull	10 cm	9 cm
Measurement of chest behind elbows	45 cm	44 cm
Length of body	43 cm	40 cm
Weight	8 kg	7 kg

- *Eyes too big or protruding.*
- *Ears too big or too small, or different in shape or carriage than described in the standard.*
- *Back too long or too short.*
- *Crooked forelegs, incorrect front.*
- *Coat too fine or too coarse.*

Pendevour Casanova at Wreckla is a beautiful representative of the breed from the UK.

DISQUALIFYING FAULTS:
- *Absence of more than 4 teeth altogether; absence of 2 or more incisors.*
- *Canine placed in vestibulo position.*
- *Entropion or ectropion.*
- *Chest circumference more than 50 cm.*
- *Curled tail or carried over the back.*
- *Long brindled coat on dogs older than 2 years.*
- *Coarse or curled cotton-wool-type hair.*
- *White markings covering more than 20%; white blaze on the head.*
- *Irregular, jerky, spasmodic movements ("Scottie cramp").*
- *Weight above 10 kg or less than 6 kg.*
- *Shyness, unbalanced or aggressive disposition.*

Note: Male animals should have two apparently normal testicles fully descended into the scrotum.

EXPLANATION OF THE FCI STANDARD
By Frantisek Horak
The Cesky Terrier was created by crossbreeding the Scottish Terrier and Sealyham Terrier. Therefore, he must be a compromise between the two breeds and it is an essential mistake to consider him as a colored Sealyham Terrier. The Cesky Terrier must not have characteristics typical of the

A dog's proper gait is a testament to his proper construction, which is why a show dog's movement is evaluated in the ring.

breeds of origin; he must always be a small, light, mobile, not-too-thick-haired dog.

The allowed height at the withers of a Cesky Terrier is between 25 and 32 cm, but experi-ence and time show that the majority of individuals are 27 to 29 cm high. As the Cesky Terrier must be lighter and more mobile than his ancestral breeds, the breed standard restricts his weight from 6 to 10 kg. Ceskies weighing more than 10 kg must not be evaluated as standard.

The Cesky Terrier's head is never as slim as the Scottish Terrier's head, but it must not be as wide as the Sealyham Terrier's head. The Cesky's eyes are always dark, smaller than the eyes of the Sealyham. The ears are V-shaped, smaller, clearly bent above the crown, well lying by the skull and carried forward. Big, hanging ears, carried at the side of the head as seen in the Sealyham Terrier, are faults.

The Cesky's bite may be either of two kinds—scissors or level bite. Both kinds are allowed and neither is preferred. The standard does not specify that a complete bite is required, but missing incisors are considered as a disqualifying fault.

The neck of the Cesky Terrier should be as long as possible, very straight and carried in a graceful

arch. The thorax is barrel-shaped (round-shaped in the cross-section) but not too deep, in order to keep room for the limbs. The front of the dog, however, must not be too wide! The back is of medium length; a minor fault is a too-long back line, as is a too-short back line. The back must not be straight and stout; it must be springy when pressed down upon. The loins are medium-vaulted, but not so much as in the Dandie Dinmont Terrier.

An important trait in the Cesky Terrier is correct tailset and carriage. The tail should be carried relatively low in an elegant lengthening of the back line. The tail can be carried higher in movement, but never curled above the back. A low-carried tail must not be seen as a sign of questionable temperament in this breed, but should be preferred.

The forelegs should be as straight as possible, and they should be set more on the sides of the body in order to be able to move freely alongside the body. Limbs situated under the body are a fault. The elbows must not protrude. The hindquarters are parallel, well angled and mobile.

The movement of the Cesky Terrier should be roomy, free, light, lively, gay; the free straight movement of the forelegs alongside the body is typical of the breed.

The Cesky Terrier can be seen in all nuances of gray, beginning

A Dutch show Cesky named Garex Alzbeta.

with nearly white (platinum blonde) to dark gray-black. White markings are allowed on up to 20% of the total body surface. Many Cesky Terriers have yellow markings on the muzzle, chest, legs, underside and under the tail. These markings are different, from nearly white to a deep rusty color. Therefore, it is not a fault for the Cesky Terrier to have yellow or a rusty color on his beard and legs.

Brown-colored Cesky Terriers exist, but this is infrequent. For these individuals, the same markings are accepted as for the gray dogs.

The coat is silky and soft, but sturdy, long and always groomed by trimming. The basic style of grooming is given in the standard. Therefore, the distinct coat style of the Cesky must be correct to complement the dog, just as is done in other breeds with distinct styles like the Kerry Blue Terrier, Bedlington Terrier or Poodle. The Cesky Terrier must always give a slim impression, emphasized by proper grooming.

The coat must not exceed the basic outline of the dog when viewed from the side, from behind and from above. Therefore, the coat must not be too abundant or too long, or, conversely, too close.

Longer, untrimmed, only slightly waved hair is on the foreface (beard and eyebrows), on the underparts of legs, on the chest

and on the belly. On the crown, on the neck and on the back, the hair is wavier, about 1.5 cm long. The cheeks, ears, throat, breast, shoulders, elbows, thighs, calves, area under the tail and tail are clipped short. The transition between the long, medium and short hair must always be smooth (above all on the flanks!). When the hair on the whole head and back is trimmed short, or when the hair is

The marvelous Agáta Vnucka z Hlubiny from the Czech Republic.

METRIC CONVERSION
The FCI breed standard explains height, weight and other important measurements in metric units. The Cesky's height and weight converted are as follows: Height at withers is between 10-12 1/2 inches, with the ideal being 11 1/2 inches for males and 10 3/4 inches for females; weight is between 13 lbs and 22 lbs. Dogs that do not fall within this weight range are disqualified from showing.

left long on the breast, elbows, flanks, thighs and calves, this is quite atypical grooming and not appropriate for the show ring.

The Cesky Terrier's disposition is not that of a typical terrier. This breed is more calm and peaceable than other terriers. Timidity is not desirable, but the breed also should not be aggressive or excessively exuberant. The Cesky Terrier is very calm, even reserved, in the exhibition ring above all.

The severe faults that can occur in the Cesky Terrier can be classified as follows:

1. Faulty gait, a consequence of a disorder (Scottie cramp);

2. Faulty type—that is, when the Cesky Terrier resembles the Sealyham Terrier, when he is solid, heavy, big, too strong and muscular, with too-long hair and weight over 10 kg. Those weighing over 10 kg must be disqualified from showing, as is

done with all breeds with specified weight limits. It is always better for the Cesky Terrier to be small and light, with the correct textured coat, than to be big and heavy, with a too-thick coat;

3. Improperly shaped and carried ears; big, heavy, hanging ears; rose ears;

4. Improper body construction—short, stout back, too vaulted back;

5. Improperly carried tail, too high and/or curled over back;

6. Stripes—only light stripes are allowed on young Ceskies in the trimmed areas; conspicuous stripes and stripes on the longer hair are unacceptable.

BETTER THAN THE AVERAGE DOG

Even though you may never show your dog, you should still read the breed standard. The breed standard tells you more than just physical specifications such as how tall your dog should be; it also describes how he should act, how he should move and what unique qualities make him a Cesky Terrier. You want a typical, handsome representative of the breed, one that people will recognize as the breed you've so carefully selected and researched. If the parents of your prospective puppy bear little or no resemblance to the dog described in the breed standard, you should keep searching!

A stunning example from the breed's homeland is Hi Dido Zláta Chara.

CESKY TERRIER

FINDING A BREEDER AND SELECTING A PUPPY

After learning about the breed's character, history and appearance, you have decided that the Cesky Terrier is the breed for you. You will not be disappointed by this remarkable companion dog, but how do you find a Cesky? Good question. Regardless of in which country you live, your hunt for a Cesky will require some research, fancy footwork and possibly travel of considerable distance. You will not find pages of advertisements in the dog periodicals, because this is a rare breed. While its following is extremely dedicated, it is also rather limited in the US at this point in time. But that is not all bad! Unlike overly popular breeds like the Labrador Retriever, Border Collie and German Shepherd, the Cesky Terrier does

XiXa Kvítko with the Garex "B" litter at just one day old.

not suffer from profiteering dealers trying to sell unsound, unhealthy puppies.

The breeders that you find for the Cesky should be dedicated to the breed and, ideally, knowledgeable about dogs in general and the breed in particular. Dedicated Cesky breeders belong to their breed club, compete at the shows and are adamant about proper socialization of their dogs. These same people are very much aware of who else in the breed does or does not ascribe to the breed club's rigid code of ethics. Do not settle for less than a reputable breeder! Here are some of the ways to find a litter of Cesky Terrier puppies:

1. Contact the secretary or registrar of the National Cesky Terrier Club of America (NCTCA), who can refer you to reputable breeders.

2. Contact the national kennel club, which should have information about puppies available by breed. Although the American Kennel Club does not yet recognize the Cesky Terrier, residents of the US have other options: contact the American Rare Breed Association, the

Portrait of a future champion: Von Guenzburg's Serena's Song as a three-month-old.

Continental Kennel Club or the United Kennel Club. These are all-breed registries that hold shows and keep track of dogs in hundreds of breeds. In Great Britain, The Kennel Club is the national club; Europeans will rely upon the Fédération Cynologique Internationale (FCI) and breed clubs in their respective countries.

3. Check in dog magazines and the weekly published dog papers. You may have to subscribe to one of these, although the more popular ones are available at newsstands and stores.

4. Go to dog shows where the breed is represented and meet the exhibitors.

5. Your local vet may be able to help.

6. The Internet is a fabulous source of information on rare

COLOR CHANGE

Cesky puppies are born black, and then turn gray, except for the very rare brown, which is born brown with a liver nose.

breeds, but always beware that there are some unscrupulous advertisers using this medium. Double-check any contacts you make online with the national breed club.

MEETING THE LITTER

Once you have done some research, met some reputable people in the breed and found an ethical breeder with a litter of Cesky pups, make arrangements to go and meet the puppies as soon as possible. Again, be prepared to travel if a suitable breeder is not located within a convenient distance. Breeders commonly allow visitors around the fifth or sixth week. During this time, you can pick out your puppy and the breeder will keep him until he is of appropriate age to go home with you (about eight to ten weeks old). Puppies at five weeks of age will be absolutely irresistible.

Be sure to meet adults of the breeder's line to get a good idea of how his pups mature in looks, soundness and temperament.

Easy does it! When you arrive at the breeder's home (and before you are seduced by the litter), look around to see how clean the premises are. Note if there is space where the puppies can be alone, to rest and sleep, or if they are crowded into a small corner.

When you first see the puppies, they should all run towards you, wanting to be fussed over. They should all be about the same size. Be wary of the one that stays in the corner, away from the others, or one that is smaller or thinner than the rest. Look at their eyes to see if any of them have runny or red bloodshot eyes; they should be bright and sparkling. If, while you are there, any pup passes movements, note that they should be dark and firm (never runny or grayish).

Ask the breeder to let you see the sire and dam. The parents will give you a good idea of what the puppies' future temperament will be. It is possible (even likely) that the sire does not live with the breeder, but the dam should always be available on the premises and the breeder should have at least photos and the pedigree of the sire.

Watch how the pups move. It should be easy to see them move straight on well-boned legs. Beware of the puppy that keeps falling over or whose legs do not move smoothly. Remember to ask the breeder if you can see copies of the parents' health certificates, which should have been obtained from the dogs' vet. If the breeder cannot supply these (or claims that they are not necessary, etc.), then you should definitely go with another breeder, no matter how adorable the puppies are! Fortunately, the Cesky is a hardy breed, and there are no health problems specific to the breed. Occasionally a case of "Scottie cramp," which causes bouts of leg spasms that subside with rest, is reported in the Cesky, due to the original crossbreeding with the Scottish Terrier, but this is rare. Affected dogs are excluded from the show ring, but the condition does not affect a Cesky's wonderful qualities as a pet.

Ask the breeder if there are any problems with the health of the parents or grandparents. A breeder who truly has the breed's best interest in mind will be willing and able to answer these questions honestly. Indeed, the breeder should be glad that you are concerned and well informed. Ask when the pups were last wormed. If one of the puppies melts your heart, pick him up for a closer examination. He should have a sweet smell. His eyes should be bright and not runny, with no signs of tear staining; his nose should be cool and moist. He should cuddle into you and appear happy and contented, but he should also be inquisitive.

A good-looking five-month-old, off to a promising start.

When you have decided on the puppy you would like to purchase, check with the breeder about the registration, insurance, a health guarantee, a list of the pup's wormings and inoculations, the pedigree, a diet sheet, a sales contract and a receipt. The breeder will allow you at least 24 hours (or more) to take the puppy to the vet for a complete examination. Make certain that the breeder will return your money or allow you to select another puppy if the vet advises you not to keep the puppy. Keep in mind that you will likely pay more for a rare-breed puppy than you will for a more popular pure-bred dog. Prices vary depending on the breeder, but you should never settle for a "bargain puppy," because you will pay for it over and over again at the vet's office—not to mention the

The best part of visiting the litter! Cuddling with the pups, of course.

be more exuberant and slower to mature, but personality is more a product of breeding and the individual pup than sex. Again, observe the parents of the litter to gauge your pup's temperament.

Of course, there are some sex-related issues, such as a male's marking territory and a female's heat cycles, which owners of show and breeding dogs must face. However, spaying the female and neutering the male saves the pet owner (and the pet) from most sexually related behavior and health issues without significantly changing the character of the breed. Spaying/neutering is recommended by vets and breeders for any dog who is not going to be shown or bred.

If the prospective owner is considering a show career for his puppy, he should be aware that the most any breeder can offer is an opinion on the "show potential" of a young puppy. Any predictions that a breeder can make about a puppy's future are based upon his experience with past litters that have produced winning show dogs. It is obvious that the more successful a breeder has been in producing winning Ceskies over the years, the broader his base of comparison will be. Give serious considera-tion to both what the standard says a show-quality Cesky must look like and the breeder's recommendations.

incalculable costs of your broken heart when the puppy succumbs to an illness or suffers from behavior problems due to an unsound temperament.

The question of male or female arises invariably when selecting a puppy. While in some breeds many differences exist between the sexes, this is not the case with the Cesky. Both make equally delightful pets, and the size difference is not significant. It is said that sometimes males can

A COMMITTED NEW OWNER

By now you should understand what makes the Cesky Terrier a most unique and special dog, one that will fit nicely into your family and lifestyle. If you have researched breeders, you should be able to recognize a knowledgeable and responsible Cesky Terrier breeder who cares not only about his pups but also about what kind of owner you will be. A good breeder will have as many questions for you as you have for him! If you have completed the final step in your new journey, you have found a litter, or possibly two, of quality Cesky Terrier pups.

A visit with the puppies and their breeder should be an education in itself. Breed research, breeder selection and puppy visitation are very important aspects of finding the puppy of your dreams. Beyond that, these things also lay the foundation for a successful future with your pup. Puppy personalities within each litter vary, from the shy and easygoing puppy to the one who is dominant and assertive, with most pups falling somewhere in between. By spending time with the puppies, you will be able to recognize certain behaviors and what these behaviors indicate about each pup's temperament. Which type of pup will complement your family dynamics is best determined by

observing the puppies in action within their "pack." Your breeder's expertise and recommendations are also

GETTING ACQUAINTED
When visiting a litter, ask the breeder for suggestions on how best to interact with the puppies. If possible, get right into the middle of the pack and sit down with them. Observe which pups climb into your lap and which ones shy away. Toss a toy for them to chase and bring back to you. It's easy to fall in love with the puppy who picks you, but keep your future objectives in mind before you make your final decision.

At five weeks old, this little guy is old enough to have visitors, but he's still a few weeks from being old enough to leave for a new home.

valuable. Although you may fall in love with a bold and brassy male, the breeder may suggest that another pup would be best for you. The breeder's experience in rearing Cesky Terrier pups and matching their temperaments with appropriate humans offers the best assurance that your pup will meet your needs and expectations. The type of puppy that you select is just as important as your decision that the Cesky Terrier is the breed for you.

The decision to live with a Cesky Terrier is a serious commitment and not one to be taken lightly. This puppy is a living sentient being that will be dependent on you for basic survival for his entire life. Beyond the basics of survival—food, water, shelter and protection—he needs much, much more. The new pup needs love, nurturing and a proper canine education to

mold him into a responsible, well-behaved canine citizen. Your Cesky Terrier's health and good manners will need consistent monitoring and regular "tune-ups," so your job as a responsible dog owner will be ongoing throughout every stage of his life. If you are not prepared to accept these responsibilities and commit to them for the next decade, likely longer, then you are not prepared to own a dog of any breed.

Although the responsibilities of owning a dog may at times tax your patience, the joy of living with your Cesky Terrier far outweighs the workload, and a well-mannered adult dog is worth your time and

A SHOW PUPPY

If you plan to show your puppy, you must first deal with a reputable breeder who shows his dogs and has had some success in the conformation ring. The puppy's pedigree should include one or more champions in the first and second generation. You should be familiar with the breed and breed standard so you can know what qualities to look for in your puppy. The breeder's observations and recommendations also are invaluable aids in selecting your future champion. If you consider an older puppy, be sure that the puppy has been properly socialized with people and not isolated in a kennel without substantial daily human contact.

effort. Before your very eyes, your new charge will grow up to be your most loyal friend, devoted to you unconditionally.

YOUR CESKY TERRIER SHOPPING LIST

Just as expectant parents prepare a nursery for their baby, so should you ready your home for the arrival of your Cesky Terrier pup. If you have the necessary puppy supplies purchased and in place before he comes home, it will ease the puppy's transition from the warmth and familiarity of his mom and littermates to the brand-new environment of his new home and human family. You will be too busy to stock up and prepare your house after your pup comes home, that's for sure! Imagine how a pup must feel upon being transported to a strange new place. It's up to you to comfort him and to let your little pup know that he is going to be happy with you.

FOOD AND WATER BOWLS

Your puppy will need separate bowls for his food and water. Stainless steel pans are generally preferred over plastic bowls since they sterilize better and pups are less inclined to chew on the metal. Heavy-duty ceramic bowls are popular, but consider how often you will have to pick up those heavy bowls. Buy adult-sized pans, as your puppy will soon grow into them.

THE DOG CRATE

If you think that crates are tools of punishment and confinement for when a dog has misbehaved, think again. Most breeders and almost all trainers recommend a crate as the preferred house-training aid as well as for all-around puppy training and safety. Because dogs are natural den creatures that prefer cave-like environments, the benefits of crate use are many. The crate provides

A sturdy crate that's big enough to comfortably house your Cesky pup when he's full-grown is a necessary initial purchase. You should have the crate before you pick up the puppy.

the puppy with his very own "safe house," a cozy place to sleep, take a break or seek comfort with a favorite toy; a travel aid to house your dog when on the road, at motels or at the vet's office; a training aid to help teach your puppy proper toileting habits; a place of solitude when non-dog people happen to drop by and don't want a lively puppy—or even a well-behaved adult dog— saying hello or begging for attention.

Crates come in several types, although the wire crate and the fiberglass airline-type crate are the most popular. Both are safe and your puppy will adjust to either one, so the choice is up to you.

The wire crates offer better visibility for the pup as well as better ventilation. Many of the wire crates easily fold down for easy transport. The fiberglass crates, similar to those used by the airlines for animal transport, are sturdier and more den-like. However, the fiberglass crates do not collapse and are less ventilated than a wire crate, which can be problematic in hot weather. Some of the newer crates are made of heavy plastic mesh; they are very lightweight and fold

The most common types of crate: mesh (left), wire (right) and fiberglass (top).

up into slim-line suitcases. However, a mesh crate might not be suitable for a pup with manic chewing habits.

Don't bother with a puppy-sized crate. Although a Cesky is not a large terrier, he will grow up in the blink of an eye and your puppy crate will be useless. Purchase a crate that will accommodate an adult Cesky Terrier. A medium-sized crate should suit him nicely. Keep in mind his adult height and length of body when considering crate measurements.

BEDDING AND CRATE PADS

Your puppy will enjoy some type of soft bedding in his "room" (the crate), something he can snuggle into to feel cozy and secure. Old towels or blankets are good choices for a young pup, since he may (and probably will) have a toileting accident or two in the crate or decide to chew on the bedding material. Once he is fully trained and out of the early chewing stage, you can replace the puppy bedding with a permanent crate pad if you prefer. Crate pads and other dog beds run the gamut from inexpensive to high-end doggie-designer styles, but don't splurge on the good stuff until you are sure that your puppy is reliable and won't tear it up or make a mess on it.

Puppy Toys

Just as infants and older children require objects to stimulate their minds and bodies, puppies need toys to entertain their curious brains, wiggly paws and achy teeth. A fun array of safe doggie toys will help satisfy your puppy's chewing instincts and distract him from gnawing on the leg of your antique chair or your new leather sofa. Most puppy toys

are cute and look as if they would be a lot of fun, but not all are necessarily safe or good for your puppy, so use caution when you go puppy-toy shopping.

Although Ceskies are not necessarily voracious chewers, they still love to chew, especially if bored and without sufficient human contact. As adults and pups, all terriers have strong teeth! The best "chewcifiers" are sturdy nylon and hard rubber bones which are safe to gnaw on and come in sizes appropriate for all age groups and breeds. Be especially careful of natural bones, which can splinter or develop dangerous sharp edges; pups can easily swallow or choke on those bone splinters. Veterinarians often tell of surgical nightmares involving bits of splintered bone, because in addition to the danger of choking, the sharp pieces can damage the intestinal tract.

Similarly, rawhide chews, while a favorite of most dogs and puppies, can be equally dangerous. Pieces of rawhide are easily swallowed after they get soft and gummy from chewing, and dogs have been known to choke on large pieces of ingested rawhide. Rawhide chews should be offered only when you can supervise the puppy.

Soft woolly toys are special puppy favorites. They come in a wide variety of cute shapes and

CONFINEMENT

It is wise to keep your puppy confined to a small "puppy-proofed" area of the house for his first few weeks at home. Gate or block off a space near the door he will use for outdoor potty trips. Expandable baby gates are useful to create puppy's designated area. If he is allowed to roam through the entire house or even only several rooms, it will be more difficult to house-train him.

sizes; some look like little stuffed animals. Puppies love to shake them up and toss them about, or simply carry them around. Be careful of fuzzy toys that have button eyes or noses that your pup could chew off and swallow, and make sure that he does not disembowel a squeaky toy to remove the squeaker! Braided rope toys are similar in that they are fun to chew and toss around, but they shred easily and the strings are easy to swallow. The strings are not digestible and, if the puppy doesn't pass them in his stool, he could end up at the vet's office. As with rawhides, your puppy should be closely monitored with rope toys.

If you believe that your pup has ingested a piece of one of his toys, check his stools for the next couple of days to see if he passes the item when he defecates. At the same time, also watch for signs of intestinal distress. A call to your veterinarian might be in order to get his advice and be on the safe side.

An all-time favorite toy for puppies (young and old!) is the empty gallon milk jug. Hard plastic juice containers—46 ounces or more—are also excellent. Such containers make lots of noise when they are batted about, and puppies go crazy with delight as they play with them. However, they don't last very long, so be sure to remove and

TOYS 'R SAFE

The vast array of tantalizing puppy is staggering. Stroll through any pet shop or pet-supply outlet and you will see that the choices can be overwhelming. However, not all dog toys are safe or sensible. Most very young puppies enjoy soft woolly toys that they can snuggle with and carry around. (You know they have outgrown them when they shred them up!) Avoid toys that have buttons, tabs or other enhancements that can be chewed off and swallowed. Soft toys that squeak are fun, but make sure your puppy does not disembowel the toy and remove (and swallow) the squeaker. Toys that rattle or make noise can excite a puppy, but they present the same danger as the squeaky kind and so require supervision. Hard rubber toys that bounce can also entertain a pup, but make sure that the toy is too big for your pup to swallow.

replace them when they get chewed up.

A word of caution about homemade toys: be careful with your choices of non-traditional play objects. Never use old shoes or socks, since a puppy cannot distinguish between the old ones on which he's allowed to chew and the new ones in your closet that are strictly off limits. That principle applies to anything that resembles something that you don't want your puppy to chew.

TOXIC PLANTS

Plants are natural puppy magnets, but many can be harmful, even fatal, if ingested by a puppy or adult dog. Scout your yard and home interior and remove any plants, bushes or flowers that could be even mildly dangerous. It could save your puppy's life. You can obtain a complete list of toxic plants from your veterinarian, at the public library or by looking online.

COLLARS

A lightweight nylon collar is the best choice for a very young pup. Quick-clip collars are easy to put on and remove, and they can be adjusted as the puppy grows. Introduce him to his collar as soon as he comes home to get him accustomed to wearing it. He'll get used to it quickly and won't mind a bit. Make sure that it is snug enough that it won't slip off, yet loose enough to be comfortable for the pup. You should be able to slip two fingers between the collar and his neck. Check the collar often, as puppies grow in spurts, and his collar can become too tight almost overnight. Choke collars are made for training, but are not always suitable for terriers and too harsh for the Cesky's sensitive temperament. Ceskies respond best to positive reinforcement and will not do well with correction-based training such as a choke collar.

LEASHES

A 6-foot nylon lead is an excellent choice for a young puppy. It is lightweight and not as tempting to chew as a leather lead. You can switch to a 6-foot leather lead after your pup has grown and is used to walking politely on a lead. For initial puppy walks and house-training purposes, you should invest in a shorter lead so that you have more control over the puppy. At first, you don't want him wandering too far away from you, and when taking him out for toileting you will want to keep him in the specific area chosen for his potty spot.

Once the puppy is heel-trained with a traditional leash, you can consider purchasing a retractable lead. A retractable lead is excellent for walking adult dogs that are already leash-wise. The retractable lead allows the dog to roam farther away from you and explore a wider area when out walking, and also retracts when you need to keep him close to you.

HOME SAFETY FOR YOUR PUPPY

The importance of puppy-proofing cannot be overstated. In addition to making your house comfortable for your Cesky Terrier's arrival, you also must make sure that your house is safe for your puppy before you bring him home. There are countless hazards in the owner's personal living environment that a pup can sniff, chew, swallow or destroy. Many are obvious; others are not. Do a thorough advance house check to remove or rearrange those things that could hurt your puppy, keeping any potentially dangerous items out of areas to which he will have access.

Electrical cords are especially dangerous, since puppies view them as irresistible chew toys. Unplug and remove all exposed

cords or fasten them beneath a baseboard where the puppy cannot reach them. Veterinarians and firefighters can tell you horror stories about electrical burns and house fires that resulted from puppy-chewed electrical cords. Consider this a most serious precaution for your puppy and the rest of your family.

Scout your home for tiny objects that might be seen at a pup's eye level. Keep medication bottles and cleaning supplies well out of reach, and do the same with waste baskets and other trash containers. It goes without saying that you should not use rodent poison or other toxic chemicals in any puppy area and that you must keep such containers safely locked up. You will be amazed at how many places a curious puppy can discover!

Once your house has cleared inspection, check your yard. The landscaping should be free of harmful pesticides, fertilizers and

A playful Cesky pup puts the squeeze on a feline housemate—"you're not leaving here until we're friends!"

A six-week-old on the prowl. A pup isn't picky when it comes to picking things up; pups must be supervised constantly to be sure they don't follow their noses into danger.

other chemicals. A sturdy fence, well embedded into the ground, will give your dog a safe place to play and potty.

Do not let a fence give you a false sense of security. With nothing else to do, the neglected Cesky can dig a hole that appears will get him to the center of the earth (terriers are the "earth dogs," remember?). Nor will the average height fence deter the Cesky if he feels there is good need for his being on the other side. A proper fence should be no less that 5–6 feet high. Check the fence periodically for necessary repairs. If there is a weak link or space to squeeze through, you can be sure a determined Cesky Terrier will discover it.

The garage and shed can be hazardous places for a pup, as things like chemicals, tools and other dangerous items are usually kept there. It's best to keep these areas off limits to the pup. Antifreeze is especially dangerous to dogs, as they find the taste appealing and it takes only a few licks from the driveway to kill a dog, puppy or adult, small breed or large.

VISITING THE VETERINARIAN
A good veterinarian is your Cesky Terrier puppy's best health-insurance policy. If you do not already have a vet, ask friends and experienced dog people in your area for recommendations so that you can select a vet before you bring your Cesky Terrier puppy home. Also arrange for your puppy's first veterinary examination beforehand, since many vets do not have appointments immediately available and your puppy should visit the vet within a day or so of coming home.

It's important to make sure that your puppy's first visit to the vet is a pleasant and positive one. The vet should take great care to befriend the pup and handle him gently to make their first meeting

---

SIGNS OF A HEALTHY PUPPY
Healthy puppies are robust little fellows who are alert and active, sporting shiny coats and supple skin. They should not appear lethargic, bloated or pot-bellied, nor should they have flaky skin or runny or crusted eyes or noses. Their stools should be firm and well formed, with no evidence of blood or mucus.

PUPPY PARASITES

Parasites are nasty little critters that live in or on your dog or puppy. Most puppies are born with ascarid roundworms, which are acquired from dormant ascarids residing in the dam. Other parasites can be acquired through contact with infected fecal matter. Take a stool sample to your vet for testing. He will prescribe a safe wormer to treat any parasites found in your puppy's stool. Always have a fecal test performed at your puppy's annual veterinary exam.

a positive experience. The vet will give the pup a thorough physical examination and set up a schedule for vaccinations and other necessary wellness visits. Be sure to show your vet any health and inoculation records, which you should have received from your breeder. Your vet is a great source of canine health information, so be sure to ask questions and take notes. Creating a health journal for your puppy will make a handy reference for his wellness and any future health problems that may arise.

MEETING THE FAMILY

Your Cesky Terrier's homecoming is an exciting time for all members of the family, and it's only natural that everyone will be eager to meet him, pet him and play with him. However, for the puppy's sake, it's best to make these initial family meetings as uneventful as possible so that the pup is not overwhelmed with too much too soon. Remember, he has just left his dam and his littermates and is away from the breeder's home for the first time. Despite his fuzzy wagging tail, he is still apprehensive and wondering where he is and who all these strange humans are and your Cesky will need a little time to warm up to all of the strange faces. It's best to let him explore on his own and meet the family members as he feels comfortable. Let him investigate all the new smells, sights and sounds at his own pace. Children should be especially careful to not get overly excited, use loud voices or hug the pup too tightly. Be calm, gentle and affectionate, and be ready to comfort him if he appears frightened or uneasy.

A promising trio of Von Guenzburg puppies at three months old: Touch of Gold (Chester), Silver Charm (Mikey) and Serena's Song (Serena).

FIRST NIGHT IN HIS NEW HOME

So much has happened in your Cesky Terrier puppy's first day away from the breeder. He's had his first car ride to his new home. He's met his new human family and perhaps the other family pets. He has explored his new house and yard, at least those places where he is to be allowed during his first weeks at home. He may have visited his new veterinarian. He has eaten his first meal or two away from his dam and littermates. Surely that's enough to tire out an eight-week-old Cesky Terrier pup...or so you hope!

It's bedtime. During the day, the pup investigated his crate, which is his new den and sleeping space, so it is not entirely strange to him. Line the crate with a soft towel or blanket that he can snuggle into and gently place him into the crate for the night. Some breeders send home a piece of

bedding from where the pup slept with his littermates, and those familiar scents are a great comfort for the puppy on his first night without his siblings.

He will probably whine or cry. The puppy is objecting to the confinement and the fact that he is alone for the first time. This can be a stressful time for you as well as for the pup. It's important that you remain strong and don't let the puppy out of his crate to comfort him. He will fall asleep eventually. If you release him, the puppy will learn that crying means "out" and will continue that habit. You are laying the groundwork for future habits. Some breeders find that soft music can soothe a crying pup and help him get to sleep.

Your puppy will miss the comforts of cuddling up with a littermate when he first comes home.

SOCIALIZING YOUR PUPPY

The first 20 weeks of your Cesky Terrier puppy's life are the most important of his entire lifetime. A properly socialized puppy will grow up to be a confident and stable adult who will be a pleasure to live with and a welcome addition to the neighborhood.

The importance of socialization cannot be overemphasized. Research on canine behavior has proven that puppies who are not exposed to new sights, sounds, people and animals during their first 20 weeks of life will grow up to be timid and fearful, even aggressive, and unable to flourish outside of their familiar home environment.

Socializing your puppy is not difficult and, in fact, will be a fun time for you both. Lead training goes hand in hand with socialization, so your puppy will be learning how to walk on a lead at

the same time that he's meeting the neighborhood. Because the Cesky Terrier is such a terrific breed, your puppy will enjoy being "the new kid on the block." Take him for short walks, to the park and to other dog-friendly places where he will encounter new people, especially children. Puppies automatically recognize children as "little people" and are drawn to play with them. Just make sure that you supervise these meetings and that the children do not get too rough or encourage him to play too hard. An overzealous pup can often nip too hard, frightening the child and in turn making the puppy overly excited. A bad experience in puppyhood can impact a dog for life, so a pup that has a negative experience with a child may grow up to be shy or even aggressive around children.

Take your puppy along on your daily errands. Puppies are

The best way to a Cesky's heart, and the best way to encourage his good behavior, is through his stomach! This five-month-old happily accepts his reward.

CREATE A SCHEDULE

Puppies thrive on sameness and routine. Offer meals at the same time each day, take him out at regular times for potty trips and do the same for play periods and outdoor activity. Make note of when your puppy naps and when he is most lively and energetic, and try to plan his day around those times. Once he is house-trained and more predictable in his habits, he will be better able to tolerate changes in his schedule.

Who can imagine that something so small, with such a sweet face, could ever cause puppy mischief?

natural "people magnets," and most people who see your pup will want to pet him. All of these encounters will help to mold him into a confident adult dog. Likewise, you will soon feel like a confident, responsible dog owner, rightly proud of your well-mannered Cesky Terrier.

Be especially careful of your puppy's encounters and experiences during the eight-to-ten-week-old period, which is also called the "fear period." This is a serious imprinting period, and all contact during this time should be gentle and positive. A frightening or negative event could leave a permanent impression that could affect his future behavior if a similar situation arises.

Also make sure that your puppy has received his first and second rounds of vaccinations before you expose him to other dogs or bring him to places that other dogs may frequent. Avoid dog parks and other strange-dog areas until your vet assures you

that your puppy is fully immunized and resistant to the diseases that can be passed between canines. Discuss socialization with your breeder, as some breeders recommend socializing the puppy even before he has received all of his inoculations, depending on how outgoing the puppy may be.

LEADER OF THE PUPPY'S PACK
Like other canines, your puppy needs an authority figure, someone he can look up to and regard as the leader of his "pack." His first pack leader was his dam, who taught him to be polite and not chew too hard on her ears or nip at her muzzle. He learned those same lessons from his littermates. If he played too rough, they cried in pain and stopped the

---

COST OF OWNERSHIP
The purchase price of your puppy is merely the first expense in the typical dog budget. Quality dog food, veterinary care (sickness and health maintenance), dog supplies and grooming costs will add up to big bucks every year. Can you adequately afford to support a canine addition to the family?

game, which sent an important message to the rowdy puppy.

As puppies play together, they are also struggling to determine who will be the boss. Being pack animals, dogs need someone to be in charge. If a litter of puppies remained together beyond puppyhood, one of the pups would emerge as the strongest one, the one who calls the shots.

Once your puppy leaves the pack, he will look intuitively for a new leader. If he does not recognize you as that leader, he will try to assume that position for himself. Of course, it is hard to imagine your adorable Cesky Terrier puppy trying to be in charge when he is so small and seemingly helpless. You must remember that these are natural canine instincts. Do not cave in and allow your pup to get the upper "paw"!

Just as socialization is so important during these first 20 weeks, so too is your puppy's early education. He was born without any bad habits. He does not know what is good or bad behavior. If he does things like nipping and digging, it's because he is having fun and doesn't know that humans consider these things as "bad." It's your job to teach him proper puppy manners, and this is the best time to accomplish that...before he has developed bad habits, since it is much more difficult to "unlearn" or correct

unacceptable learned behavior than to teach good behavior from the start.

Make sure that all members of the family understand the importance of being consistent when training their new puppy. If you tell the puppy to stay off the sofa and your daughter allows him to cuddle on the couch to watch her favorite television show, your pup will be confused about what he is and is not allowed to do. Have a family conference before your pup comes home so that everyone understands the basic principles of puppy training and the rules you have set forth for the pup, and agrees to follow them.

The old saying that "an ounce of prevention is worth a pound of cure" is especially true when it comes to puppies. It is much easier to prevent inappropriate behavior than it is to change it. It's also easier and less stressful for the pup, since it will keep discipline to a minimum and create a more positive learning environment for him. That, in turn, will also be easier on you!

SOLVING PUPPY PROBLEMS

CHEWING AND NIPPING
Nipping at fingers and toes is normal puppy behavior. Chewing is also the way that puppies investigate their surroundings. However, you will have to teach

To a teething pup, everything tastes like relief. If it's within reach, it will likely end up in his mouth.

your puppy that chewing anything other than his toys is not acceptable. That won't happen overnight and at times puppy teeth will test your patience. However, if you allow nipping and chewing to continue, just think about the damage that a mature Cesky Terrier can do with a full set of adult terrier teeth.

Whenever your puppy nips your hand or fingers, cry out "Ouch!" in a loud voice, which should startle your puppy and stop him from nipping, even if only for a moment. Immediately distract him by offering a small treat or an appropriate toy for him to chew instead (which means having chew toys and puppy treats handy or in your pockets at all times). Praise him when he takes the toy and tell him what a good fellow he is. Praise is just as or even more important in puppy training as discipline and correction.

Puppies also tend to nip at children more often than adults, since they perceive little ones to be more vulnerable and more similar to their littermates. Teach your children appropriate responses to nipping behavior. If they are unable to handle it themselves, you may have to intervene. Puppy nips can be quite painful and a child's frightened reaction will only encourage a puppy to nip harder, which is a natural canine response. As with all other puppy situations, interaction between your Cesky Terrier puppy and children should be supervised.

Chewing on objects, not just family members' fingers and ankles, is also normal canine behavior that can be especially tedious (for the owner, not the pup) during the teething period when the puppy's adult teeth are coming in. At this stage, chewing just plain feels good. Furniture legs and cabinet corners are common puppy favorites. Shoes and other personal items also taste pretty good to a pup.

The best solution is, once again, prevention. If you value something, keep it tucked away and out of reach. You can't hide your dining-room table in a closet, but you can try to deflect the chewing by applying a bitter product made just to deter dogs from chewing. Available in a spray or cream, this substance is vile-tasting, although safe for dogs, and most puppies will avoid the forbidden object after one tiny taste. You also can apply the product to your leather leash if the puppy tries to chew on his lead during leash-training sessions.

Keep a ready supply of safe chews handy to offer your Cesky Terrier as a distraction when he starts to chew on something that's a "no-no." Remember, at this tender age he does not yet know what is permitted or forbidden, so you have to be "on call" every minute he's awake and on the prowl.

You may lose a treasure or two during puppy's growing-up period, and the furniture could sustain a nasty nick or two. These can be trying times, so be prepared for those inevitable accidents and comfort yourself in knowing that this too shall pass.

PUPPY WHINING

Puppies often cry and whine, just as infants and little children do. It's their way of telling us that they are lonely or in need of attention. Your puppy will miss his littermates and will feel insecure when he is left alone. You may be out of the house or just in another room, but he will still feel alone. During these times, the puppy's crate should be his personal comfort station, a place all his own where he can feel safe and secure. Once he learns that being alone is okay and not something to be feared, he will settle down without crying or objecting. You might want to leave a radio on while he is crated, as the sound of human voices can be soothing and will give the impression that people are around.

Give your puppy a favorite cuddly toy or chew toy to entertain him whenever he is crated. You will both be happier: the puppy because he is safe in his den and you because he is quiet, safe and not getting into puppy escapades that can wreak havoc in your house or cause him danger.

To make sure that your puppy will always view his crate as a safe and cozy place, never, *ever*, use the crate as punishment. That's the best way to turn the crate into a negative place that the pup will want to avoid. Sure, you can use the crate for your own peace of mind if your puppy is getting into trouble and needs some "time out." Just don't let him know that! Never scold the pup and immediately place him into the crate. Count to ten, give him a couple of hugs and maybe a treat, then scoot him into his crate.

It's also important not to make a big fuss when he is released from the crate. That will make getting out of the crate more appealing than being in the crate, which is just the opposite of what you are trying to achieve.

DIET DON'TS

- Got milk? Don't give it to your dog! Dogs cannot tolerate large quantities of cows' milk, as they do not have the enzymes to digest lactose.
- You may have heard of dog owners who add raw eggs to their dogs' food for a shiny coat or to make the food more palatable, but consumption of raw eggs too often can cause a deficiency of the vitamin biotin.
- Avoid feeding table scraps, as they will upset the balance of the dog's complete food. Additionally, fatty or highly seasoned foods can cause upset canine stomachs.
- Do not offer raw meat to your dog. Raw meat can contain parasites; it also is high in fat.
- Vitamin A toxicity in dogs can be caused by too much raw liver, especially if the dog already gets enough vitamin A in his balanced diet, which should be the case.
- Bones like chicken, pork chop and other soft bones are not suitable, as they easily splinter.

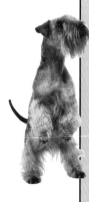

FEEDING

Feeding your dog the best diet is based on various factors, including age, activity level, overall condition and size of the breed. When you visit the breeder, he will share with you his advice about the proper diet for your dog based on his experience with the breed and the foods with which he has had success. Likewise, your vet will be a helpful source of advice throughout the dog's life and will aid you in planning a diet for optimal health.

FEEDING THE PUPPY

Of course, your pup's very first food will be his dam's milk. There may be special situations in which pups fail to nurse, necessitating that the breeder hand-feed them with a formula, but for the most part pups spend the first weeks of life nursing from their dam. The breeder weans the pups by gradually introducing solid foods and decreasing the milk meals. Pups may even start themselves off on the weaning process, albeit

VEGGIE DOGS

Ceskies love to eat fruit and veggies like frozen peas, baby raw carrots and apples. They also eat and digest grass. Are they vegetarians? No! But they do enjoy many foods that other dogs may not.

inadvertently, if they snatch bites from their mom's food bowl.

By the time the pups are ready for new homes, they are fully weaned and eating a good puppy food. As a new owner, you may be thinking, "Great! The breeder has taken care of the hard part." Not so fast.

A puppy's first year of life is the time when all or most of his growth and development takes place. This is a delicate time, and diet plays a huge role in proper skeletal and muscular formation. Improper diet and exercise habits can lead to damaging problems that will compromise the dog's health and movement for his entire life. That being said, new owners should not worry needlessly. With the myriad types of food formulated specifically for growing pups of different-sized breeds, dog-food manufacturers have taken much of the guesswork out of feeding your puppy well. Since growth-food formulas are designed to provide the nutrition that a growing puppy needs, it is unnecessary and, in fact, can prove harmful to add supplements

to the diet. Research has shown that too much of certain vitamin supplements and minerals predispose a dog to skeletal problems. It's by no means a case of "if a little is good, a lot is better." At every stage of your dog's life, too much or too little in the way of nutrients can be harmful, which is why a manufactured complete food is the easiest way to know that your dog is getting what he needs.

Because of a young pup's small body and accordingly small digestive system, his daily portion will be divided up into small meals throughout the day. This can mean starting off with three or more meals a day and decreasing the number of meals as the pup matures. It is generally thought that dividing the adult dog's daily food into two meals on a

By nursing from their mother, these one-week-old pups are getting the best possible nutrition for their stage of life.

At six weeks old, a
pup will be eating
solid foods at
least for some of
his meals as part
of the weaning
process.

morning/evening schedule is healthier for the dog's digestion than one large meal.

Regarding the feeding schedule, feeding the pup at the same times and in the same place each day is important for both housebreaking purposes and establishing the dog's everyday routine. As for the amount to feed, growing puppies generally need proportionately more food per body weight than their adult counterparts, but a pup should never be allowed to gain excess weight. Dogs of all ages should be kept in proper body condition, but extra weight can strain a pup's developing frame, causing skeletal problems.

Watch your pup's weight as he grows and, if the recommended amounts seem to be too much or too little for your pup, consult the vet about appropriate dietary changes. Keep in mind that treats, although small, can quickly add up throughout the day, contributing unnecessary calories. Treats are fine when used prudently; opt for dog treats specially formulated to be healthy or for nutritious snacks like small pieces of cheese or cooked chicken.

FEEDING THE ADULT DOG

For the adult (meaning physically mature) dog, feeding properly is about maintenance, not growth.

Again, correct weight is a concern. Your dog should appear fit and should have an evident "waist." His ribs should not be protruding (a sign of being underweight), but they should be covered by only a slight layer of fat. Under normal circumstances, an adult dog can be maintained fairly easily with a high-quality nutritionally complete adult-formula food. However, it is important to know that Ceskies truly love to eat and won't stop on their own, so watch the portion control.

Factor treats into your dog's overall daily caloric intake, and avoid offering table scraps. Certain "people foods," like chocolate, onions, nuts, grapes and raisins, are toxic to dogs. Plus, you don't want to encourage begging or overeating. Overweight dogs are more prone to health problems. Research has even shown that obesity takes years off a dog's life. With that in mind, resist the urge to overfeed and over-treat. Don't make unnecessary additions to your dog's diet, whether with tidbits or with extra vitamins and minerals.

The amount of food needed for proper maintenance will vary depending on the individual dog's activity level, but you will be able to tell whether the daily portions are keeping him in good shape. With the wide variety of good complete foods available, choosing what to feed is largely a matter of personal preference. Just as with the puppy, the adult dog should have consistency in his mealtimes and feeding place. In addition to a consistent routine, regular mealtimes also allow the owner to see how much his dog is eating. If the dog seems never to be satisfied or, likewise, becomes uninterested in his food, the owner will know right away that something is wrong and can consult the vet.

DIETS FOR THE AGING DOG

A good rule of thumb is that once a dog has reached 75% of his expected lifespan, he has reached "senior citizen" or geriatric status. Your Cesky Terrier will be considered a senior at about 8 years of age; he has a projected lifespan of about 12–14 years. (The smallest breeds generally enjoy the longest lives and the largest breeds the shortest.)

HOLD THE ONIONS

Sliced, chopped or grated; dehydrated, boiled, fried or raw; pearl, Spanish, white or red: onions can be deadly to your dog. The toxic effects of onions in dogs are cumulative for up to 30 days. A serious form of anemia, called Heinz body anemia, affects the red blood cells of dogs that have eaten onions. For safety (and better breath), dogs should avoid chives and scallions as well.

At five months old, this pup's growing frame needs complete and balanced nutrition formulated for healthy, not rapid, growth.

What does aging have to do with your dog's diet? No, he won't get a discount at the local diner's early-bird special. Yes, he will require some dietary changes to accommodate the changes that come along with increased age. One change is that the older dog's dietary needs become more similar to that of a puppy. Specifically, dogs can metabolize more protein as youngsters and seniors than in the adult-maintenance stage. Discuss with your vet whether you need to switch to a higher-protein or senior-formulated food or whether your current adult-dog food contains sufficient nutrition for the senior.

Watching the dog's weight remains essential, even more so in the senior stage. Older dogs are already more vulnerable to illness,

and obesity only contributes to their susceptibility to problems. As the older dog becomes less active and thus exercises less, his regular portions may cause him to gain weight. At this point, you may consider decreasing his daily food intake or switching to a reduced-calorie food. As with other changes, you should consult your vet for advice.

DON'T FORGET THE WATER!
For a dog, it's always time for a drink! Regardless of what type of food he eats, there's no doubt that he needs plenty of water. Fresh cold water, in a clean bowl, should be freely available to your dog at all times. There are special

NOT HUNGRY?
No dog in his right mind would turn down his dinner, would he? If you notice that your dog has lost interest in his food, there could be any number of causes. Dental problems are a common cause of appetite loss, one that is often overlooked. If your dog has a toothache, a loose tooth or sore gums from infection, chances are it doesn't feel so good to chew. Think about when you've had a toothache! If your dog does not approach the food bowl with his usual enthusiasm, look inside his mouth for signs of a problem. Whatever the cause, you'll want to consult your vet so that your chow hound can get back to his happy, hungry self as soon as possible.

circumstances, such as during puppy housebreaking, when you will want to monitor your pup's water intake so that you will be able to predict when he will need to relieve himself, but water must be available to him nonetheless. Water is essential for hydration and proper body function just as it is in humans.

You will get to know how much your dog typically drinks in a day. Of course, in the heat or if exercising vigorously, he will be more thirsty and will drink more. However, if he begins to drink noticeably more water for no apparent reason, this could signal any of various problems, and you are advised to consult your vet.

Water is the best drink for dogs. Some owners are tempted to give milk from time to time or to moisten dry food with milk, but dogs do not have the enzymes necessary to digest the lactose in milk, which is much different from the milk that nursing puppies receive. Therefore, stick with clean fresh water to quench your dog's thirst, and always have it readily available to him.

EXERCISE

We all know the importance of exercise for humans, so it should come as no surprise that it is essential for our canine friends as well. Now, regardless of your own level of fitness, get ready to assume the role of personal

trainer for your dog. It's not as hard as it sounds, and it will have health benefits for you, too.

Just as with anything else you do with your dog, you must set a routine for his exercise. It's the same as your daily morning run before work or never missing the 7 p.m. aerobics class. If you plan it and get into the habit of actually doing it, it will become just another part of your day. Think of it as making daily exercise appointments with your dog, and stick to your schedule.

As a rule, dogs in normal health should have at least a half-hour of activity each day. Dogs with health or orthopedic problems may have specific limitations, so their exercise plans are best devised with the help of a vet. For healthy dogs, there are many ways to fit 30 minutes of

A thirsty puppy! No matter what life stage, water is always an important component of a healthy dog's diet.

Don't let too many treats undo the good in your Cesky's balanced diet and regular activity.

and play sessions in the yard are good for a growing pup, and his exercise can be increased as he grows up.

For overweight dogs, dietary changes and activity will help the goal of weight loss. (Sound familiar?) While they should of course be encouraged to be active, remember not to overdo it, as the excess weight is already putting strain on his vital organs and bones. As for highly active dogs, some of them never seem to tire! They will enjoy time spent with their owners doing things together.

Regardless of your dog's condition and activity level, exercise offers benefits to all dogs and owners. Consider the fact that dogs who are kept active are more stimulated both physically and mentally, meaning that they are less likely to become bored and lapse into destructive behavior. Also consider the benefits of one-on-one time with your dog every day, continually strengthening the bond between the two of you. Furthermore, exercising together will improve health and longevity for both of you. You both need exercise, and now you and your dog have a workout partner and motivator!

activity into your day. Depending on your schedule, you may plan a 15-minute walk or activity session in the morning and again in the evening, or do it all at once in a half-hour session each day. Walking is the most popular way to exercise a dog (it's good for you, too!); other suggestions include retrieving games, jogging and disc-catching or other active games with his toys. If you have a safe body of water nearby and a dog that likes to swim, swimming is an excellent form of exercise for dogs, putting no stress on his frame.

On that note, some precautions should be taken with a puppy's exercise. During his first year, when he is growing and developing, your Cesky Terrier should not be subject to vigorous activity that stresses his body. Short walks at a comfortable pace

GROOMING THE CESKY
Potential Cesky owners should be prepared to commit some time to grooming their dogs. We start our

puppies with a daily brushing, using a natural pure bristle brush. Frequent grooming is important for puppies, as the softer puppy coat is more prone to matting than the adult coat. Basic coat care should be done three to four times a week (once weekly is the absolute minimum). With the dog lying on his back, use either a "universal slicker" or a pin brush (sharp ends), brushing first with the growth of the hair and then against the growth of the hair. Then brush the legs in the same manner. Using a metal comb, gently comb through the underbelly and the legs, thus removing any tangles or mats.

With regard to the larger mats, a spritz of detangling coat spray

The "fall" is brushed forward. This is a breed trademark, as the hair over the eyes is intended for protection.

Be gentle when brushing the facial furnishings, as you don't want your Cesky to associate grooming with pain. He will be much more tolerant of the process if he feels comfortable.

The leg furnishings are brushed out to achieve the desired "bell" shape.

GROOMING TOOLS:

- Fine-toothed comb
- Bristle brush
- Universal slicker
- Mat breaker
- Thinning shears/scissors
- Electric clippers with blades 7F, 10 and 30
- Anti-matting lotion
- Ear-cleansing powder or liquid
- Cotton pads
- Hemostats, to pull ear hair
- Canine toothpaste and toothbrush for dental care
- Nail clippers
- Shampoo and conditioner formulated for dogs
- Towels and blow dryer

forehead

stop

ankle

The general Cesky trim. The ankle is the guide for trimming the lower outline while the stop is the guide for the facial regions.

The hair on the forehead (shaded area) should be 1.5 cm long.

chest

The hair on the shaded area should be 1.5 cm long.

elbow

The bottom of the legs should have the shape of a bell.

It is very important that the shorter areas and longer areas blend together.

can help to comb them out. Using a "mat breaker," combing away from the skin, also helps to remove the mats. In worst-case scenarios, the mats can be cut out with scissors, saving as much of the long hair as possible. The usual site for mats to form is under the legs (or the "armpits," if you will). Finish with an overall brushing of the body and face.

If it's time to trim your Cesky, you can begin to do so once the dog is brushed and combed out and mat-free; then you can begin the basic trim. The Cesky is trimmed, even for show purposes, not hand-stripped like other terrier breeds. For the basic trim, use your electric clippers with the #7 fine blade. Start at eye level and trim toward the tail, leaving skirting on line from the front legs to the back legs. Trim the chest from the neck to below the legs, leaving long hair on the lower chest to blend with the long hair on the legs. The face is trimmed, leaving the "fall" (long hair) over the front of the face and the beard.

Check trimming sketches as you go along. Many Cesky owners groom and trim their own dogs, and diagrams are available to help. The beard can be thinned, using thinning scissors, to be neat and tidy. Ears are trimmed inside and out with a #30 blade. Trim the edges of the ears as close as possible to the "leathers" with

Take a lesson from a groomer or your breeder before attempting to clip your Cesky yourself. Terrier grooming is an art that requires learning and practice.

The longer hair under the belly must be given extra attention, as this area is more prone to matting, tangling and picking up debris.

After brushing through the furnishings, finish up with a comb to ensure that there are no mats or tangles.

straight scissors. The legs can be trimmed (again, consult a grooming diagram to see how this should look) using the #10 blade. The tail is also trimmed using the #10 blade. The groin area is tidied up with the #7 fine blade for hygiene.

For a show dog, the show trim is very similar. Show dogs should have a basic trim six weeks before the show. One week before the show, you should redo the tail, face, throat and ears. Also, consult a grooming diagram to do the legs. Shampoo and blow dry. As a rule,

WATER SHORTAGE

No matter how well behaved your dog is, bathing is always a project! Nothing can substitute for a good warm bath, but owners do have the option of giving their dogs "dry" baths. Pet shops sell excellent products, in both powder and spray forms, designed for spot-cleaning your dog. These dry shampoos are convenient for touch-up jobs when you don't have the time to bathe your dog in the traditional way.

Muddy feet, messy behinds and smelly coats can be spot-cleaned and deodorized with a "wet-nap"-style cleaner. On those days when your dog insists on rolling in fresh goose droppings and there's no time for a bath, a spot bath can save the day. These pre-moistened wipes are also handy for other grooming needs like wiping faces, ears and eyes and freshening tails and behinds.

baths can be given at the same time as the trim, usually every six to eight weeks, unless the need arises sooner. For a show dog, this may vary depending on the show schedule.

An important rule of grooming your Cesky: never cut the "fall"! This is the basic look of the Cesky Terrier. Its purpose is to protect the eyes when walking or hunting in the forest.

BATHING

If you give your dog his first bath when he is young, he will become accustomed to the process. Wrestling a dog into the tub or chasing a freshly shampooed dog who has escaped from the bath will be no fun! Most dogs don't naturally enjoy their baths, but you at least want yours to cooperate with you.

Before bathing the dog, have the items you'll need close at hand. First, decide where you will bathe the dog. You should have a tub or basin with a non-slip surface. Small dogs can even be bathed in a sink. In warm weather, some like to use a portable pool in the yard, although you'll want to make sure your dog doesn't head for the nearest dirt pile following his bath! You will also need a hose or shower spray to wet the coat thoroughly, a shampoo formulated for dogs, absorbent towels and a blow dryer (you can buy one made for dogs or use your own on the lowest heat). Human shampoos are too harsh for dogs' coats and will dry them out.

Before wetting the dog, give him a brush-through to remove any dead hair, dirt and mats. Make sure he is at ease in the tub and have the water at a comfortable temperature. Begin bathing by wetting the coat all the way down to the skin. Massage in the shampoo, keeping it away from his face and eyes. Rinse him thoroughly, again avoiding the eyes and ears, as you don't want to get water into the ear canals. A thorough rinsing is important, as shampoo residue is drying and itchy to the dog. After rinsing, wrap him in a towel to absorb the initial moisture. You can finish with a blow dryer on low heat, held at a safe distance from the dog. You should keep the dog indoors and away from drafts until he is completely dry.

NAIL CLIPPING

Having his nails trimmed is not on many dogs' lists of favorite things to do. With this in mind, you will need to accustom your puppy to the procedure at a young age so that he will sit still (well, as still as he can) for his pedicures. Long nails can cause the dog's feet to spread, which is not good for him; likewise, long nails can hurt if they unintentionally scratch, not good for you!

Some dogs' nails are worn down naturally by regular walking on hard surfaces, so the frequency with which you clip depends on your individual dog. Look at his nails from time to time and clip as needed; a good way to know when it's time for a trim is if you hear your dog clicking as he walks across the floor.

There are several types of nail clippers and even electric nail-grinding tools made for dogs; first we'll discuss using the clipper. To start, have your clipper ready and some doggie treats on hand. You want your pup to view his nail-clipping sessions in a positive light, and what better way to convince him than with food? You may want to enlist the help of an assistant to comfort the pup and offer treats as you concentrate on the clipping itself. The guillotine-

Nail clippers made for dogs are available at most pet-supply shops. If you want an adult Cesky who behaves well for his pedicures, start the nail-clipping routine when he is a pup.

type clipper is thought of by many as the easiest type to use; the nail tip is inserted into the opening, and blades on the top and bottom snip it off in one clip.

Start by grasping the pup's paw; a little pressure on the foot pad causes the nail to extend, making it easier to clip. Clip off a little at a time. If you can see the "quick," which is a blood vessel that runs through each nail, you will know how much to trim, as you do not want to cut into the quick. On that note, if you do cut the quick, which will cause bleeding, you can stem the flow of blood with a styptic pencil or other clotting agent. If you mistakenly nip the quick, do not panic or fuss, as this will cause the pup to be afraid. Simply reassure the pup, stop the bleeding and move on to the next nail. Don't be discouraged; you will become a professional canine pedicurist with practice.

You may or may not be able to see the quick, so it's best to just clip off a small bit at a time. If you see a dark dot in the center of the nail, this is the quick and your cue to stop clipping. Tell the puppy he's a "good boy" and offer a piece of treat with each nail. You can also use nail-clipping time to examine the footpads, making sure that they are not dry and cracked and that nothing has become embedded in them.

The nail grinder, the second choice, is many owners' first choice. Accustoming the puppy to the sound of the grinder and sensation of the buzz presents fewer challenges than the clipper, and there's no chance of cutting through the quick. Use the grinder

THE MONTHLY GRIND

If your dog doesn't like the feeling of nail clippers or if you're not comfortable using them, you may wish to try an electric nail grinder. This tool has a small sandpaper disc on the end that rotates to grind the nails down. Some feel that using a grinder reduces the risk of cutting into the quick; this can be true if the tool is used properly. Usually you will be able to tell where the quick is before you get to it. A benefit of the grinder is that it creates a smooth finish on the nails so that there are no ragged edges.

Because the tool makes noise, your dog should be introduced to it before the actual grinding takes place. Turn it on and let your dog hear the noise; turn it off and let him inspect it with you holding it. Use the grinder gently, holding it firmly and progressing a little at a time until you reach the proper length. Look at the nail as you grind so that you do not go too short. Stop at any indication that you are nearing the quick. It will take a few sessions for both you and the puppy to get used to the grinder. Make sure that you don't let his hair get tangled in the grinder.

on a low setting and always talk soothingly to your dog. He won't mind his salon visit, and he'll have nicely polished nails as well.

EAR CLEANING

While keeping your dog's ears clean unfortunately will not cause him to "hear" your commands any better, it will protect him from ear infection and ear-mite infestation. In addition, a dog's ears are vulnerable to waxy build-up and to collecting foreign matter from the outdoors. Look in your dog's ears regularly to ensure that they look pink, clean and otherwise healthy. Even if they look fine, an odor in the ears signals a problem and means it's time to call the vet.

A dog's ears should be cleaned regularly; once a week is suggested, and you can do this along with your regular brushing. Using a cotton ball or pad, and never probing into the ear canal, wipe the ear gently. You can use an ear-cleansing liquid or powder available from your vet or pet-supply store; alternatively, you might prefer to use home-made solutions with ingredients like one part white vinegar and one part hydrogen peroxide. Ask your vet about home remedies before you attempt to concoct something on your own!

Keep your dog's ears free of excess hair by plucking it as needed. If done gently, this will

be painless for the dog. Look for wax, brown droppings (a sign of ear mites), redness or any other abnormalities. At the first sign of a problem, contact your vet so that he can prescribe an appropriate medication.

Make ear cleaning part of the grooming routine, using soft cotton and an ear-cleaning product from your vet or the pet shop.

EYE CARE

During grooming sessions, pay extra attention to the condition of your dog's eyes. If the area around the eyes is soiled or if tear staining has occurred, there are various cleaning agents made especially for this purpose. Look at the dog's eyes to make sure no debris has entered; dogs with large eyes and those who spend time outdoors are especially prone to this, but the Cesky has the advantage of the fall over his eyes, intended to protect them.

teeth and checking his overall oral condition. Studies show that around 80% of dogs experience dental problems by two years of age, and the percentage is higher in older dogs. Therefore, it is highly likely that your dog will have trouble with his teeth and gums unless you are proactive with home dental care.

The most common dental problem in dogs is plaque build-up. If not treated, this causes gum disease, infection and resultant tooth loss. Bacteria from these infections spread throughout the body, affecting the vital organs. Do you need much more convincing to start brushing your dog's teeth? If so, take a good whiff of your dog's breath, and read on.

Fortunately, home dental care is rather easy and convenient for pet owners. Specially formulated canine toothpaste is easy to find. You should use one of these toothpastes, not a product for humans. Some doggie pastes are even available in flavors appealing to dogs. If your dog likes the flavor, he will tolerate the process better, making things much easier for you! Doggie toothbrushes come in different sizes and are designed to fit the contour of a canine mouth. Rubber fingertip brushes fit right on one of your fingers and have rubber nodes to clean the teeth and massage the gums. This may

The area around the eyes can be wiped to remove any dirt or debris that may have collected there. There are also products available for removing tear stains.

The signs of an eye infection are obvious: mucus, redness, puffiness, scabs or other signs of irritation. If your dog's eyes become infected, the vet will likely prescribe an antibiotic ointment for treatment. If you notice signs of more serious problems, such as opacities in the eye, which usually indicate cataracts, consult the vet at once. Taking time to pay attention to your dog's eyes will alert you in the early stages of any problem so that you can get your dog treatment as soon as possible. You could save your dog's sight!

A CLEAN SMILE

Another essential part of grooming is brushing your dog's

be easier to handle, as it is akin to rubbing your dog's teeth with your finger.

As with other grooming tasks, accustom your Cesky Terrier pup to his dental care early on. Start gently, for a few minutes at a time, so that he gets used to the feel of the brush and to your handling his mouth. Offer praise and petting so that he looks at tooth-care time as a time when he gets extra love and attention. The routine should become second nature; he may not like it, but he should at least tolerate it.

Aside from brushing, offer dental toys to your dog and feed crunchy biscuits, which help to minimize plaque. Rope toys have the added benefit of acting like floss as the dog chews. At your adult dog's yearly check-ups, the vet will likely perform a thorough tooth scraping as well as a complete check for any problems. Proper care of your dog's teeth will ensure that you will enjoy your dog's smile for many years to come. The next time your dog goes to give you a hello kiss, you'll be glad you spent the time caring for his teeth.

THE OTHER END

Dogs sometime have troubles with their anal glands, which are sacs located beside the anal vent. These should empty when a dog has normal bowel movements; if

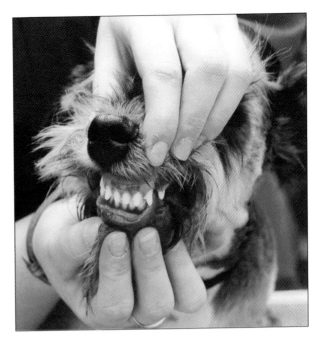

they don't, they can become full or impacted, causing discomfort. Owners often are alarmed to see their dogs scooting across the floor, dragging their behinds behind, but this is just a dog's attempt to empty the glands himself.

Some brave owners attempt to evacuate their dogs' anal glands themselves during grooming, but no one will tell you that this is a pleasant task! Thus, many owners prefer to make the trip to the vet to have the vet take care of the problem; owners whose dogs visit a groomer can have this done by the groomer if he offers this as part of his services. Regardless, don't neglect the dog's other end

A healthy mouth is the gateway to overall internal health. Dogs need regular dental care throughout their lives, just as we do.

in your home-care routine. Look for scooting, licking or other signs of discomfort "back there" to ascertain whether the anal glands need to be emptied.

IDENTIFICATION AND TRAVEL

ID FOR YOUR DOG

You love your Cesky Terrier and want to keep him safe. Of course, you take every precaution to prevent his escaping from the yard or becoming lost or stolen. You have a sturdy high fence and you always keep your dog on lead when out and about in public places. If your dog is not properly identified, however, you are overlooking a major aspect of his safety. We hope to never be in a situation where our dog is missing, but we should practice prevention in the unfortunate case that this happens; identification greatly increases the chances of your dog's being returned to you

There are several ways to identify your dog. First, the traditional dog tag should be a staple in your dog's wardrobe, attached to his everyday collar. Tags can be made of sturdy plastic and various metals and should include your contact information so that a person who finds the dog can get in touch with you right away to arrange his return. Many people today enjoy the wide range of decorative tags available, so have fun and create a tag to match

your dog's personality. Of course, it is important that the tag stays on the collar, so have a secure "O" ring attachment; you also can explore the type of tag that slides right onto the collar.

In addition to the ID tag, which every dog should wear even if identified by another method, two other forms of identification have become popular: microchipping and tattooing. In microchipping, a tiny scannable chip is painlessly inserted under the dog's skin. The number is registered to you so that, if your lost dog turns up at a clinic or shelter, the chip can be scanned to retrieve your contact information.

The advantage of the microchip is that it is a permanent form of ID, but there are some factors to consider. Several different companies make

---

PET OR STRAY?
Besides the obvious benefit of providing your contact information to whoever finds your lost dog, an ID tag makes your dog more approachable and more likely to be recovered. A strange dog wandering the neighborhood without a collar and tags will look like a stray, while the collar and tags indicate that the dog is someone's pet. Even if the ID tags become detached from the collar, the collar alone will make a person more likely to pick up the dog.

microchips, and not all are compatible with the others' scanning devices. It's best to find a company with a universal microchip that can be read by scanners made by other companies as well. It won't do any good to have the dog chipped if the information cannot be retrieved. Also, not every humane society, shelter and clinic is equipped with a scanner, although more and more facilities are equipping themselves. In fact, many shelters microchip dogs that they adopt out to new homes.

In the US, there are five or six major microchip manufacturers as well as a few databases. The American Kennel Club's Companion Animal Recovery unit works in conjunction with HomeAgain™ Companion Animal Retrieval System (Schering-Plough). In the UK, The Kennel Club is affiliated with the National Pet Register, operated by Wood Green Animal Shelters.

Because the microchip is not visible to the eye, the dog must wear a tag that states that he is microchipped so that whoever picks him up will know to have him scanned. He of course also should have a tag with contact information in case his chip cannot be read. Humane societies and veterinary clinics offer microchipping service, which is usually very affordable.

Though less popular than microchipping, tattooing is another permanent method of ID for dogs. Most vets perform this service, and there are also clinics that perform dog tattooing. This is also an affordable procedure and one that will not cause much discomfort for the dog. It is best to put the tattoo in a visible area, such as the ear, to deter theft. It is sad to say that there are cases of dogs' being stolen and sold to research laboratories, but such laboratories will not accept tattooed dogs.

To ensure that the tattoo is effective in aiding your dog's return to you, the tattoo number must be registered with a national organization. That way, when someone finds a tattooed dog, a phone call to the registry will quickly match the dog with his owner.

Whether traveling across town or across the country, your dog's collar, ID tags and leash are necessary for his safety.

HIT THE ROAD

Car travel with your Cesky Terrier may be limited to necessity only, such as trips to the vet, or you may bring your dog along almost everywhere you go. This will depend much on your individual dog and how he reacts to rides in the car. You can begin desensitizing your dog to car travel as a pup so that it's something that he's used to. Still, some dogs suffer from motion sickness. Your vet may prescribe a medication for this if trips in the car pose a problem for your dog. At the very least, you will need to get him to the vet, so he will need to tolerate these trips with the least amount of hassle possible.

Start taking your pup on short trips, maybe just around the block to start. If he is fine with short trips, lengthen your rides a little at a time. Start to take him on your errands or just for drives around town. By this time, it will be easy to tell whether your dog is a born traveler or would prefer staying at home when you are on the road.

Of course, safety is a concern for dogs in the car. First, he must travel securely, not left loose to roam about the car where he could be injured or distract the driver. A young pup can be held by a passenger initially but should soon graduate to a travel crate, which can be the same crate he uses in the home. Other options include a car harness (like a seat belt for dogs) and partitioning the back of the car with a gate made for this purpose.

Bring along what you will need for the dog. He should wear his collar and ID tags, of course, and you should bring his leash, water (and food if a long trip) and clean-up materials for potty breaks and in case of motion sickness. Always keep your dog on his leash when you make stops, and never leave him alone in the car. Many a dog has died from the heat inside a closed car; this does not take much time at all. A dog left alone inside a car can also be a target for thieves.

UP, UP AND AWAY!

Taking a trip by air does not mean that your dog cannot accompany you, it just means that you will have to be well informed and well prepared. The majority of dogs travel as checked cargo; only the smallest of breeds are allowed in the cabin with their owners. Your dog must travel in an airline-approved travel crate appropriate to his size so that he will be safe and comfortable during the flight. If the crate that you use at home does not meet the airline's specifications, you can purchase one from the airline or from your pet-supply store (making sure it is labeled as airline-approved).

It's best to have the crate in advance of your trip to give the dog time to get accustomed to it.

Here is the preferred mode of transport for Von Guenzburg puppies Charismatic (Archie) and Secretariat (Sammy).

You can put a familiar blanket and a favorite toy or two in the crate with the dog to make him feel at home and to keep him occupied. The crate should be lined with absorbent material for the trip, with bowls for food and water attached to the outside of the crate. The crate must be labeled with your contact information, feeding instructions and a statement asserting that the dog was fed within a certain time frame of arrival at the airport (check with your airline). You will also have to provide proof of current vaccinations.

Again, advance planning is the key to smooth sailing in the skies. Make your reservations well ahead of time and know what restrictions your airline imposes: no travel during certain months, refusal of certain breeds, restrictions on certain destinations. In spite of all of these variables, major carriers have much experience with transporting animals, so have a safe flight!

DOG-FRIENDLY DESTINATIONS
When planning vacations, a question that often arises is, "Who will watch the dog?" More and more families, however, are answering that question with, "We will!" With the rise in dog-friendly places to visit, the number of families who bring their dogs along on vacation is on

Many of today's boarding kennels offer specialized services in addition to basic upkeep.

the rise. A search online for dog-friendly vacation spots will turn up many choices, as well as resources for owners of canine

DOGGONE!

Wendy Ballard is the editor and publisher of the *DogGone*™ newsletter, which comes out bi-monthly and features fun articles by dog owners who love to travel with their dogs. The newsletter includes information about fun places to go with your dog, including popular vacation spots, dog-friendly hotels, parks, campgrounds, resorts, etc., as well as interesting activities to do with your dog, such as flyball, agility and much more. You can subscribe to the publication by contacting the publisher at PO Box 651155, Vero Beach, FL 32965-1155.

travelers. Ask others for suggestions: your vet, your breeder, other dog owners, breed club members, people at the local doggie day care.

Traveling with your Cesky Terrier means providing for his comfort and safety, and you will have to pack a bag for him just as you do for yourself (although you probably won't have liver treats in your own suitcase!). Bring his everyday items: food, water, bowls, leash and collar (with ID!), brush and comb, toys, bed, crate, plus any additional accessories that he will need once you get to your vacation spot. If he takes medication, don't forget to bring it with you. If going camping or on another type of outdoor excursion, make sure that your dog is protected from ticks, mosquitoes and other pests. Above all, have a good time with your dog and enjoy each other's company!

BOARDING

Today there are many options for dog owners who need someone to care for their dogs in certain circumstances. While many think of boarding their dogs as something to do when away on vacation, many others use the services of doggie "daycare" facilities, dropping their dogs off to spend the day while they are at work. Many of these facilities offer both long-term and daily care. Many go beyond just boarding and cater to all sorts of needs, with on-site grooming, veterinary care, training classes and even "web-cams" where owners can log onto the internet and check out what their dogs are up to. Most dogs enjoy the activity and time spent with other dogs.

Before you need to use such a service, check out the ones in your area. Make visits to see the facilities, meet the staff, discuss fees and available services and see whether this is a place where you think your dog will be happy. It is best to do your research in advance so that you're not stuck at the last minute, forced into making a rushed decision without knowing whether the kennel that you've chosen meets your standards. You also can check with your vet's office to see

whether they offer boarding for their clients or can recommend a good kennel in the area.

The kennel will need to see proof of your dog's health records and vaccinations so as not to spread illness from dog to dog. Your dog also will need proper identification. Owners usually experience some separation anxiety the first time they have to leave their dog in someone else's care, so it's reassuring to know that the kennel you choose is run by experienced, caring, true dog people.

KEEP OFF THE GRASS

As a conscientious dog owner, you never use fertilizers, pesticides or other harmful landscaping chemicals. However, you cannot expect everyone in your neighborhood to do the same. When out walking your dog, it is best to stay on sidewalks and not to allow your dog to explore the neighbors' front lawns; of course, this is for your dog's safety as well as for maintaining good rapport with the neighbors. Highly tailored yards are danger zones, and many (but not all) lawn services put up signs or flags to warn others of recently treated grass. Also beware of unfamiliar grassy areas when traveling. Dogs can absorb these chemicals through their feet or ingest them if they lick their paws following walks. To be on the safe side, rinse or wipe down your dog's feet each time you come in from a walk.

TRAINING YOUR
CESKY TERRIER

BASIC TRAINING PRINCIPLES: PUPPY VS. ADULT

There's a big difference between training an adult dog and training a young puppy. With a young puppy, everything is new. At eight to ten weeks of age, he will be experiencing many things, and he has nothing with which to compare these experiences. Up to this point, he has been with his dam and littermates, not one-on-one with people except in his interactions with his breeder and visitors to the litter.

When you first bring the puppy home, he is eager to please you. This means that he accepts doing things your way. During the next couple of months, he will absorb the basis of everything he needs to know for the rest of his life. This early age is even referred to as the "sponge" stage. After that, for the next 18 months, it's up to you to reinforce good manners by building on the foundation that you've established. Once your puppy is reliable in basic commands and behavior and has reached the appropriate age, you may gradually introduce him to some of the interesting sports, games and activities available to pet owners and their dogs.

Raising your puppy is a family affair. Each member of the family must know what rules to set forth for the puppy and how to use the same one-word commands to mean exactly the same thing every time. Even if yours is a large family, one person will soon be considered by the pup to be the leader, the Alpha person in his pack, the "boss" who must be obeyed. Often that highly regarded person turns out to be the one who feeds the puppy. Food ranks

Your little bundle of joy! Read on to learn how to mold him into a companion with whom you will have a rewarding friendship throughout his life.

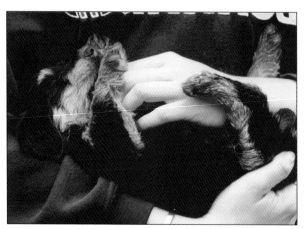

very high on the puppy's list of important things! That's why your puppy is rewarded with small treats along with verbal praise when he responds to you correctly. As the puppy learns to do what you want him to do, the food rewards are gradually eliminated and only the praise remains. If you were to keep up with the food treats, you could have two problems on your hands—an obese dog and a beggar.

Training begins the minute your Cesky Terrier puppy steps through the doorway of your home, so don't make the mistake of putting the puppy on the floor and telling him by your actions to "Go for it! Run wild!" Even if this is your first puppy, you must act as if you know what you're doing: be the boss. An uncertain pup may be terrified to move, while a bold one will be ready to take you

A youngster will follow the leader; he wants to be near you and to please you. Take advantage of this stage of his life, when his potential for learning is at its peak.

at your word and start plotting to destroy the house! Before you collected your puppy, you decided where his own special place would be, and that's where to put him when you first arrive home. Give him a house tour after he has investigated his area and had a nap and a bathroom "pit stop."

It's worth mentioning here that, if you've adopted an adult dog that is completely trained to your liking, lucky you! You're off the hook! However, if that dog spent his life up to this point in a kennel, or even in a good home

SHOULD WE ENROLL?

If you have the means and the time, you should definitely take your dog to obedience classes. Begin with Puppy Kindergarten Classes in which puppies of all sizes learn basic lessons while getting the opportunity to meet and greet each other; it's as much about socialization as it is about good manners. What you learn in class you can practice at home. And if you goof up in practice, you'll get help in the next session.

CANINE DEVELOPMENT SCHEDULE

It is important to understand how and at what age a puppy develops into adulthood. If you are a puppy owner, consult the following Canine Development Schedule to determine the stage of development your puppy is currently experiencing. This knowledge will help you as you work with the puppy in the weeks and months ahead.

PERIOD	AGE	CHARACTERISTICS
FIRST TO THIRD	BIRTH TO SEVEN WEEKS	Puppy needs food, sleep and warmth and responds to simple and gentle touching. Needs mother for security and disciplining. Needs littermates for learning and interacting with other dogs. Pup learns to function within a pack and learns pack order of dominance. Begin socializing pup with adults and children for short periods. Pup begins to become aware of his environment.
FOURTH	EIGHT TO TWELVE WEEKS	Brain is fully developed. Pup needs socializing with outside world. Remove from mother and littermates. Needs to change from canine pack to human pack. Human dominance necessary. Fear period occurs between 8 and 12 weeks. Avoid fright and pain.
FIFTH	THIRTEEN TO SIXTEEN WEEKS	Training and formal obedience should begin. Less association with other dogs, more with people, places, situations. Period will pass easily if you remember this is pup's change-to-adolescence time. Be firm and fair. Flight instinct prominent. Permissiveness and over-disciplining can do permanent damage. Praise for good behavior.
JUVENILE	FOUR TO EIGHT MONTHS	Another fear period about 7 to 8 months of age. It passes quickly, but be cautious of fright and pain. Sexual maturity reached. Dominant traits established. Dog should understand sit, down, come and stay by now.

NOTE: THESE ARE APPROXIMATE TIME FRAMES. ALLOW FOR INDIVIDUAL DIFFERENCES IN PUPPIES.

but without any real training, be prepared to tackle the job ahead. A dog three years of age or older with no previous training cannot be blamed for not knowing what he was never taught. While the dog is trying to understand and learn your rules, at the same time he has to unlearn many of his previously self-taught habits and general view of the world.

Working with a professional trainer will speed up your progress with an adopted adult dog. You'll need patience, too. Some new rules may be close to impossible for the dog to accept. After all, he's been successful so far by doing everything his way! (Patience again.) He may agree with your instruction for a few days and then slip back into his old ways, so you must be just as consistent and understanding in your teaching as you would be with a puppy. (More patience needed yet again!) Your dog has to learn to pay attention to your voice, your family, the daily routine, new smells, new sounds and, in some cases, even a new climate.

One of the most important things to find out about a newly adopted adult dog is his reaction to children (yours and others), strangers and your friends, and how he acts upon meeting other dogs. If he was not socialized with dogs as a puppy, this could be a major problem. This does not mean that he's a "bad" dog, a

Your Cesky pup's crate is the most important tool in housebreaking. Once he's out of the crate, it's time to "go" in a hurry!

vicious dog or an aggressive dog; rather, it means that he has no idea how to read another dog's body language. There's no way for him to tell whether the other dog is a friend or foe. Survival instinct takes over, telling him to attack first and ask questions later. This definitely calls for professional help and, even then, may not be a behavior that can be corrected 100% reliably (or even at all). If you have a puppy, this is why it is so very important to introduce your young puppy properly to other puppies and "dog-friendly" adult dogs.

All creatures, however, respond favorably to gentle motivational methods and sincere praise and encouragement; this is especially true with the soft-tempered, gentle Cesky. The Cesky is sensitive and eager to please, and thrives on positive reinforcement. Now let us get started.

HOUSE-TRAINING YOUR CESKY TERRIER

Dogs are "touch sensitive" when it comes to house-training. In other words, they respond to the surface on which they are given approval to eliminate. The choice is yours (the dog's version is in parentheses): The lawn (including the neighbors' lawns)? A bare patch of earth under a tree (where people like to sit and relax in the summertime)? Concrete steps or patio (all sidewalks, garages and basement floors)? The curbside (watch out for cars)? A small area of crushed stone in a corner of the yard (mine!)? The latter is the best choice if you can manage it, because it will remain strictly for the dog's use and is easy to keep clean.

You can start out with paper-training indoors and switch over to an outdoor surface as the puppy matures and gains control over his need to eliminate. For the naysayers, don't worry—this won't mean that the dog will soil on every piece of newspaper lying around the house. You are training him to go outside, remember? Starting out by paper-training often is the only choice for a city dog.

WHEN YOUR PUPPY'S "GOT TO GO"

Your puppy's need to relieve himself is seemingly non-stop, but signs of improvement will be seen each week. From 8 to 10 weeks old, the puppy will have to be taken outside every time he wakes up, about 10–15 minutes after every meal and after every period of play—all day long, from first thing in the morning until his bedtime! That's a total of ten or more trips per day to teach the puppy where it's okay to relieve himself. With that schedule in mind, you can see that house-training a young puppy is not a part-time job. It requires someone to be home all day.

If that seems overwhelming or impossible, do a little planning. For example, plan to pick up your

---

POTTY COMMAND

Most dogs love to please their masters; there are no bounds to what dogs will do to make their owners happy. The potty command is a good example of this theory. If toileting on command makes the master happy, then more power to him. Puppies will obligingly piddle if it really makes their keepers smile. Some owners can be creative about which word they will use to command their dogs to relieve themselves. Some popular choices are "Potty," "Tinkle," "Piddle," "Let's go," "Hurry up" and "Toilet." Give the command every time your puppy goes into position and the puppy will begin to associate his business with the command.

puppy at the start of a vacation period. If you can't get home in the middle of the day, plan to hire a dog-sitter or ask a neighbor to come over to take the pup outside, feed him his lunch and then take him out again about ten or so minutes after he's eaten. Also make arrangements with that or another person to be your "emergency" contact if you have to stay late on the job. Remind yourself—repeatedly—that this hectic schedule improves as the puppy gets older.

HOME WITHIN A HOME

Your Cesky Terrier puppy needs to be confined to one secure, puppy-proof area when no one is able to watch his every move. Generally the kitchen is the place of choice because the floor is washable. Likewise, it's a busy family area that will accustom the pup to a variety of noises, everything from pots and pans to the telephone, blender and dishwasher. He will also be enchanted by the smell of your cooking (and will never be critical when you burn something). An exercise pen (also called an "ex-pen," a puppy version of a playpen) within the room of choice is an excellent means of confinement for a young pup. He can see out and has a certain amount of space in which to run about, but he is safe from dangerous things like electrical cords, heating units, trash baskets

DAILY SCHEDULE
How many relief trips does your puppy need per day? A puppy up to the age of 14 weeks will need to go outside about 8 to 12 times per day! You will have to take the pup out any time he starts sniffing around the floor or turning in small circles, as well as after naps, meals, games and lessons or whenever he's released from his crate. Once the puppy is 14 to 22 weeks of age, he will require only 6 to 8 relief trips. At the ages of 22 to 32 weeks, the puppy will require about 5 to 7 trips. Adult dogs typically require 4 relief trips per day, in the morning, afternoon, evening and late at night.

or open kitchen-supply cabinets. Place the pen where the puppy will not get a blast of heat or air conditioning.

In the pen, you can put a few toys, his bed (which can be his crate if the dimensions of pen and crate are compatible) and a few

LEASH TRAINING

House-training and leash training go hand in hand, literally. When taking your puppy outside to do his business, lead him there on his leash. Unless an emergency potty run is called for, do not whisk the puppy up into your arms and take him outside. If you have a fenced yard, you have the advantage of letting the puppy loose to go out, but it's better to put the dog on the leash and take him to his designated place in the yard until he is reliably house-trained. Taking the puppy for a walk is the best way to house-train a dog. The dog will associate the walk with his time to relieve himself, and the exercise of walking stimulates the dog's bowels and bladder. Dogs that are not trained to relieve themselves on a walk may hold it until they get back home, which of course defeats half the purpose of the walk.

layers of newspaper in one small corner, just in case. A water bowl can be hung at a convenient height on the side of the ex-pen so it won't become a splashing pool for an innovative puppy. His food dish can go on the floor, near but not under the water bowl.

Crates are something that pet owners are at last getting used to for their dogs. Wild or domestic canines have always preferred to sleep in den-like safe spots, and that is exactly what the crate provides. How often have you seen adult dogs that choose to sleep under a table or chair even though they have full run of the house? It's the den connection.

In your "happy" voice, use the word "Crate" every time you put the pup into his den. If he's new to a crate, toss in a small biscuit for him to chase the first few times. At night, after he's been outside, he should sleep in his crate. The crate may be kept in his designated area at night or, if you want to be sure to hear those wake-up yips in the morning, put the crate in a corner of your bedroom. However, don't make any response whatsoever to whining or crying. If he's completely ignored, he'll settle down and get to sleep.

Good bedding for a young puppy is an old folded bath towel or an old blanket, something that is easily washable and disposable if necessary ("accidents" will

SOMEBODY TO BLAME

House-training a puppy can be frustrating for the puppy and the owner alike. The puppy does not instinctively understand the difference between defecating on the pavement outside and on the ceramic tile in the kitchen. He is confused and frightened by his human's exuberant reactions to his natural urges. The owner, arguably the more intelligent of the duo, is also frustrated that he cannot convince his puppy to obey his commands and instructions.

In frustration, the owner may struggle with the temptation to discipline the puppy, scold him or even strike him on the rear end. These harsh corrections are totally inapppropriate and will also defeat your purpose in gaining your puppy's trust and respect. Don't blame your nine-week-old puppy. Blame yourself for not being 100% consistent in the puppy's lessons and routine. The lesson here is simple: try harder and your puppy will succeed.

happen!). Never put newspaper in the puppy's crate. Also, those old ideas about adding a clock to replace his mother's heartbeat, or a hot-water bottle to replace her warmth, are just that—old ideas. The clock could drive the puppy nuts, and the hot-water bottle could end up as a very soggy waterbed! An extremely good breeder would have introduced your puppy to the crate by letting two pups sleep together for a couple of nights, followed by several nights alone. How thankful you will be if you found that breeder!

Safe toys in the pup's crate or area will keep him occupied, but monitor their condition closely. Discard any toys that show signs of being chewed to bits. Squeaky parts, bits of stuffing or plastic or any other small pieces can cause intestinal blockage or possibly choking if swallowed.

PROGRESSING WITH POTTY-TRAINING

After you've taken your puppy out and he has relieved himself in the area you've selected, he can have some free time with the family as long as there is someone responsible for watching him. That doesn't mean just someone in the same room who is watching TV or busy on the computer, but one person who is doing nothing other than keeping an eye on the

Scoping out a target! Upright objects, such as potted plants, may become targets of a male dog's leg-lifting.

pup, playing with him on the floor and helping him understand his position in the pack.

This first taste of freedom will let you begin to set the house rules. If you don't want the dog on the furniture, now is the time to prevent his first attempts to jump up onto the couch. The word to use in this case is "Off," not "Down." "Down" is the word you will use to teach the down position, which is something entirely different.

Most corrections at this stage come in the form of simply distracting the puppy. Instead of telling him "No" for "Don't chew the carpet," distract the chomping puppy with a toy and he'll forget about the carpet.

As you are playing with the pup, do not forget to watch him closely and pay attention to his body language. Whenever you see him begin to circle or sniff, take the puppy outside to relieve

Once trained to a specific area, your Cesky will follow his nose to use the same spot consistently.

> ### CREATURES OF HABIT
> Canine behaviorists and trainers aptly describe dogs as "creatures of habit," meaning that dogs respond to structure in their daily lives and welcome a routine. Do not interpret this to mean that dogs enjoy endless repetition in their training sessions. Dogs get bored just as humans do. Keep training sessions interesting and exciting. Vary the commands and the locations in which you practice. Give short breaks for play in between lessons. A bored student will never be the best performer in the class.

himself. If you are paper-training, put him back into his confined area on the newspapers. In either case, praise him as he eliminates while he actually is in the act of relieving himself. Three seconds after he has finished is too late! You'll be praising him for running toward you, or picking up a toy or whatever he may be doing at that moment, and that's not what you want to be praising him for. Timing is a vital tool in all dog training. Use it.

Remove soiled newspapers immediately and replace them with clean ones. You may want to take a small piece of soiled paper and place it in the middle of the new clean papers, as the scent will attract him to that spot when it's time to go again. That scent attraction is why it's so important to clean up any messes made in

the house by using a product specially made to eliminate the odor of dog urine and droppings. Regular household cleansers won't do the trick. Pet shops sell the best pet deodorizers. Invest in the largest container you can find.

Scent attraction eventually will lead your pup to his chosen spot outdoors; this is the basis of outdoor training. When you take your puppy outside to relieve himself, use a one-word command such as "Outside" or "Go-potty" (that's one word to the puppy!) as you pick him up and attach his leash. Then put him down in his area. If for any reason you can't carry him, snap the leash on

quickly and lead him to his spot. Now comes the hard part—hard for you, that is. Just stand there until he urinates and defecates. Move him a few feet in one direction or another if he's just sitting there looking at you, but remember that this is neither playtime nor time for a walk. This is strictly a business trip! Then, as he circles and squats (remember your timing!), give him a quiet "Good dog" as praise. If you start to jump for joy, ecstatic over his performance, he'll do one of two things: either he will stop mid-stream, as it were, or he'll do it again for you—in the house—and expect you to be just as delighted!

Give him five minutes or so and, if he doesn't go in that time, take him back indoors to his confined area and try again in another ten minutes, or immediately if you see him sniffing and circling. By careful observation, you'll soon work out a successful schedule.

Part of training means picking a suitable toilet area—an out-of-the-way spot in the yard is certainly preferable.

EXTRA! EXTRA!

The headlines read: "Puppy Piddles Here!" Breeders commonly use newspapers to line their whelping pens, so puppies learn to associate newspapers with relieving themselves. Do not use newspapers to line your pup's crate, as this will signal to your puppy that it is OK to urinate in his crate. If you choose to paper-train your puppy, you will layer newspapers on a section of the floor near the door he uses to go outside. You should encourage the puppy to use the papers to relieve himself, and bring him there whenever you see him getting ready to go. Little by little, you will reduce the size of the newspaper-covered area so that the puppy will learn to relieve himself "on the other side of the door."

Accidents, by the way, are just that—accidents. Clean them up quickly and thoroughly, without comment, after the puppy has been taken outside to finish his business and then put back into his area or crate. If you witness an accident in progress, say "No!" in a stern voice and get the pup outdoors immediately. No punishment is needed. You and your puppy are just learning each other's language, and sometimes it's easy to miss a puppy's message. Chalk it up to experience and watch more closely from now on.

KEEPING THE PACK ORDERLY

Discipline is a form of training that brings order to life. For example, military discipline is what allows the soldiers in an army to work as one. Discipline is a form of teaching and, in dogs, is the basis of how the successful pack operates. Each member knows his place in the pack and all respect the leader, or Alpha dog. It is essential for your puppy that you establish this type of relationship, with you as the Alpha, or leader. It is a form of social coexistence that all canines recognize and accept. Discipline, therefore, is never to be confused with punishment. When you teach your puppy how you want him to behave, and he behaves properly and you praise him for it, you are disciplining him with a form of positive reinforcement.

For a dog, rewards come in the form of praise, a smile, a cheerful tone of voice, a few friendly pats or a rub of the ears. Rewards are also small food treats. Obviously, that does not mean bits of regular dog food. Instead, treats are very small bits of special things like cheese or pieces of soft dog treats. The idea is to reward the dog with something very small that he can taste and swallow, providing instant positive reinforcement. If he has to take time to chew the treat, by the time he is finished he will have forgotten what he did to earn it!

Your puppy should never be physically punished. The displeasure shown on your face and in your voice is sufficient to signal to the pup that he has done

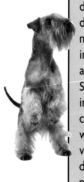

SMILE WHEN YOU ORDER ME AROUND!

While trainers recommend practicing with your dog every day, it's perfectly acceptable to take a "mental health day" off. It's better not to train the dog on days when you're in a sour mood. Your bad attitude or lack of interest will be sensed by your dog, and he will respond accordingly. Studies show that dogs are well tuned in to their humans' emotions. Be conscious of how you use your voice when talking to your dog. Raising your voice or shouting will only erode your dog's trust in you as his trainer and master.

something wrong. He wants to please everyone higher up on the social ladder, especially his leader, so a scowl and harsh voice will take care of the error. Growling out the word "Shame!" when the pup is caught in the act of doing something wrong is better than the repetitive "No." Some dogs hear "No" so often that they begin to think it's their name! By the way, do not use the dog's name when you're correcting him. His name is reserved to get his attention for something pleasant about to take place.

There are punishments that have nothing to do with you. For example, your dog may think that chasing cats is one reason for his existence. You can try to stop it as much as you like but without success, because it's such fun for the dog. But one good hissing, spitting, swipe of a cat's claws

across the dog's nose will put an end to the game forever. Intervene only when your dog's eyeball is seriously at risk. Cat scratches can cause permanent damage to an innocent but annoying puppy.

PUPPY KINDERGARTEN

COLLAR AND LEASH
Before you begin your Cesky Terrier puppy's education, he must be used to his collar and leash. Choose a collar for your puppy that is secure, but not heavy or bulky. He won't enjoy training if he's uncomfortable. A flat buckle collar is fine for everyday wear and for initial puppy training. For older dogs, there are several types of training collars such as the martingale, which is a double loop that tightens slightly around the neck, or the head collar, which is similar to a horse's halter. The

Your puppy must be used to his collar and lead before beginning with the basic commands. Initially, all exercises will be taught with the pup on lead.

BE UPSTANDING!

You are the dog's leader. During training, stand up straight so your dog looks up at you, and therefore up *to* you. Say the command words distinctly, in a clear, declarative tone of voice. (No barking!) Give rewards only as the correct response takes place (remember your timing!). Praise, smiles and treats are "rewards" used to positively reinforce correct responses. Don't repeat a mistake. Just change to another exercise—you will soon find success!

How best to get your Cesky's attention? With a tasty morsel, of course! It's a tried-and-true trick of handlers and trainers everywhere.

training class, suggestions will be made as to the best collar and leash for your young puppy. I say "wise" because your puppy will be in a class with puppies in his age range (up to five months old) of all breeds and sizes. It's the perfect way for him to learn the right way (and the wrong way) to interact with other dogs as well as their people. You cannot teach your puppy how to interpret another dog's sign language. For a first-time puppy owner, these socialization classes are invaluable. For experienced dog owners, they are a real boon to further training.

ATTENTION

You've been using the dog's name since the minute you collected him from the breeder, so you should be able to get his attention by saying his name—with a big smile and in an excited tone of voice. His response will be the puppy equivalent of "Here I am! What are we going to do?" Your immediate response (if you haven't guessed by now) is "Good dog." Rewarding him at the

chain choke collar is not recommended for the Cesky Terrier. It is neither suitable nor necessary.

A lightweight 6-foot woven cotton or nylon training leash is preferred by most trainers because it is easy to fold up in your hand and comfortable to hold because there is a certain amount of give to it. There are lessons where the dog will start off 6 feet away from you at the end of the leash. The leash used to take the puppy outside to relieve himself is shorter because you don't want him to roam away from his area. The shorter leash will also be the one to use when you walk the puppy.

If you've been wise enough to enroll in a Puppy Kindergarten

"SCHOOL" MODE

When is your puppy ready for a lesson? Maybe not always when you are. Attempting training with treats just before his mealtime is asking for disaster. Notice what times of day he performs best and make that Fido's school time.

moment he pays attention to you teaches him the proper way to respond when he hears his name.

EXERCISES FOR A BASIC CANINE EDUCATION

THE SIT EXERCISE

There are several ways to teach the puppy to sit. The first one is to catch him whenever he is about to sit and, as his backside nears the floor, say "Sit, good dog!" That's positive reinforcement and, if your timing is sharp, he will learn that what he's doing at that second is connected to your saying "Sit" and that you think he's clever for doing it!

Another method is to start with the puppy on his leash in front of you. Show him a treat in the palm of your right hand. Bring your hand up under his nose and, almost in slow motion, move your hand up and back so his nose goes up in the air and his head tilts back as he follows the treat in your hand. At that point, he will have to either sit or fall over, so as his back legs buckle under, say "Sit, good dog," and then give him the treat and lots of praise. You may have to begin with your hand lightly running up his chest, actually lifting his chin up until he sits. Some (usually older) dogs require gentle pressure on their hindquarters with the left hand, in which case the dog should be on your left side. Puppies

> ### A SIMPLE "SIT"
> When you command your dog to sit, use the word "Sit." Do not say "Sit down," as your dog will not know whether you mean "Sit" or "Down," or maybe you mean both. Be clear in your instructions to your dog; use one-word commands and always be consistent.

generally do not appreciate this physical dominance.

After a few times, you should be able to show the dog a treat in the open palm of your hand, raise your hand waist-high as you say "Sit" and have him sit. You will thereby have taught him two things at the same time. Both the verbal command and the motion of the hand are signals for the sit. Your puppy is watching you almost more than he is listening to you, so what you do is just as important as what you say.

Don't save any of these drills only for training sessions. Use them as much as possible at odd times during a normal day. The dog should always sit before being given his food dish. He should sit to let you go through a doorway first, when the doorbell rings or when you stop to speak to someone on the street.

THE DOWN EXERCISE

Before beginning to teach the down command, you must consider how the dog feels about this exercise. To him, "down" is a submissive position. Being flat on the floor with you standing over him is not his idea of fun. It's up to you to let him know that, while it may not be fun, the reward of your approval is worth his effort.

Start with the puppy on your left side in a sit position. Hold the leash right above his collar in your left hand. Have an extra-special treat, such as a small piece of cooked chicken or hot dog, in

A reluctant Cesky may need some guidance into the down position. Be gentle and reassuring to show him that there's nothing to be hesitant about.

> **KEY PRINCIPLES OF DOG TRAINING**
> 1. Start training early. A young puppy is ready, willing and able.
> 2. Timing is your all-important tool. Praise at the exact time that the dog responds correctly. Pay close attention.
> 3. Patience is almost as important as timing!
> 4. Repeat! The same word has to mean the same thing every time.
> 5. In the beginning, praise all correct behavior verbally, along with treats and petting.

your right hand. Place it at the end of the pup's nose and steadily move your hand down and forward along the ground. Hold the leash to prevent a sudden lunge for the food. As the puppy goes into the down position, say "Down" very gently.

The difficulty with this exercise is twofold: it's both the submissive aspect and the fact that most people say the word "Down" as if they were a drill sergeant in charge of recruits! So issue the command sweetly, give him the treat and have the pup maintain the down position for several seconds. If he tries to get up immediately, place your hands on his shoulders and press down gently, giving him a very quiet "Good dog." As you progress with this lesson, increase the "down time" until he will hold it until you say "Okay" (his cue for release). Practice this one in the house at various times throughout the day.

By increasing the length of time during which the dog must maintain the down position, you'll find many uses for it. For example, he can lie at your feet in the vet's office or anywhere that both of you have to wait, when you are on the phone, while the family is eating and so forth. If you progress to training for competitive obedience, he'll already be all set for the exercise called the "long down."

THE STAY EXERCISE

You can teach your Cesky Terrier to stay in the sit, down and stand positions. To teach the sit/stay, have the dog sit on your left side. Hold the leash at waist level in your left hand and let the dog know that you have a treat in your

Teaching the stay is more effective when hand signals are used along with the verbal command.

closed right hand. Step forward on your right foot as you say "Stay." Immediately turn and stand directly in front of the dog, keeping your right hand up high so he'll keep his eye on the treat hand and maintain the sit position for a count of five. Return to your original position and offer the reward.

Increase the length of the sit/stay each time until the dog can hold it for at least 30 seconds without moving. After about a week of success, move out on your right foot and take two steps before turning to face the dog. Give the "Stay" hand signal (left palm back toward the dog's head) as you leave. He gets the treat when you return and he holds the sit/stay. Increase the distance that you walk away from him before turning until you reach the length of your training leash. But don't rush it! Go back to the beginning

---

OKAY!

This is the signal that tells your dog that he can quit whatever he was doing. Use "Okay" to end a session on a correct response to a command. (Never end on an incorrect response.) Lots of praise follows. People use "Okay" a lot and it has other uses for dogs, too. Your dog is barking. You say, "Okay! Come!" "Okay" signals him to stop the barking activity and "Come" allows him to come to you for a "Good dog."

if he moves before he should. No matter what the lesson, never be upset by having to back up for a few days. The repetition and practice are what will make your dog reliable in these commands. It won't do any good to move on to something more difficult if the command is not mastered at the easier levels. Above all, even if you do get frustrated, never let your puppy know! Always keep a positive, upbeat attitude during training, which will transmit to your dog for positive results.

The down/stay is taught in the same way once the dog is completely reliable and steady with the down command. Again, don't rush it. With the dog in the down position on your left side, step out on your right foot as you say "Stay." Return by walking around in back of the dog and into your original position. While you are training, it's okay to murmur something like "Hold on" to encourage him to stay put. When the dog will stay without moving when you are at a distance of 3 or 4 feet, begin to increase the length of time before you return. Be sure he holds the down on your return until you say "Okay." At that point, he gets his treat—just so he'll remember for next time that it's not over until it's over.

THE COME EXERCISE

No command is more important to the safety of your Cesky Terrier than "Come." It is what you should say every single time you see the puppy running toward you: "Binky, come! Good dog." During playtime, run a few feet away from the puppy and turn and tell him to "Come" as he is already running to you. You can go so far as to teach your puppy two things at once if you squat down and hold out your arms. As the pup gets close to you and you're saying "Good dog," bring your right arm in about waist high. Now he's also learning the hand signal, an excellent device should you be on the phone when you need to get him to come to you! You'll also both be one step ahead when you enter obedience classes.

When the puppy responds to your well-timed "Come," try it with the puppy on the training leash. This time, catch him off guard, while he's sniffing a leaf or watching a bird: "Binky, come!" You may have to pause for a split second after his name to be sure you have his attention. If the puppy shows any sign of confusion, give the leash a mild jerk and take a couple of steps backward. Do not repeat the command. In this case, you should say "Good come" as he reaches you.

That's the number-one rule of training. Each command word is given just once. Anything more is nagging. You'll also notice that all commands are one word only.

Even when they are actually two words, you say them as one.

Never call the dog to come to you—with or without his name—if you are angry or intend to correct him for some misbehavior. When correcting the pup, you go to him. Your dog must always connect "Come" with something pleasant and with your approval; then you can rely on his response.

Puppies, like children, have notoriously short attention spans, so don't overdo it with any of the training. Keep each lesson short. Break it up with a quick run around the yard or a ball toss, repeat the lesson and quit as soon as the pup gets it right. That way, you will always end with a "Good dog."

However, life isn't perfect and neither are puppies. A time will come, often around 10 months of age, when he'll become "selectively deaf" or choose to "forget" his name. He may respond by wagging his tail (and even seeming to smile at you) with a look that says "Make me!" Laugh, throw his favorite toy and skip the lesson you had planned. Pups will be pups!

THE HEEL EXERCISE

The second most important command to teach, after the come, is the heel. When you are walking your growing puppy, you need to be in control. Besides, it looks terrible to be pulled and yanked

COME AND GET IT!
The come command is your dog's safety signal. Until he is 99% perfect in responding, don't use the come command if you cannot enforce it. Practice on leash with treats or squeakers, or whenever the dog is running to you. Never call him to come to you if he is to be corrected for a misdemeanor. Reward the dog with a treat and happy praise whenever he comes to you.

down the street, and it's not much fun either. Your eight-to ten-week-old puppy will probably follow you everywhere, but that's his natural instinct, not your control over the situation. However, any time he does follow you, you can say "Heel" and be ahead of the game, as he will learn to associate this command with the action of following you before you even begin teaching him to heel.

There is a very precise, almost military, procedure for teaching your dog to heel. As with all other

LET'S GO!

Many people use "Let's go" instead of "Heel" when teaching their dogs to behave on lead. It sounds more like fun! When beginning to teach the heel, whatever command you use, always step off on your left foot. That's the one next to the dog, who is on your left side, in case you've forgotten. Keep a loose leash. When the dog pulls ahead, stop, bring him back and begin again. Use treats to guide him around turns.

obedience training, begin with the dog on your left side. He will be in a very nice sit and you will have the training leash across your chest. Hold the loop and folded leash in your right hand. Pick up the slack leash above the dog in your left hand and hold it loosely at your side. Step out on your left foot as you say "Heel." If the puppy does not move, give a gentle tug or pat your left leg to get him started. If he surges ahead of you, stop and pull him back gently until he is at your side. Tell him to sit and begin again.

Walk a few steps and stop while the puppy is correctly beside you. Tell him to sit and give mild verbal praise. (More enthusiastic praise will encourage him to think the lesson is over.) Repeat the lesson, increasing the number of steps you take only as long as the dog is heeling nicely beside you. When you end the lesson, have him hold the sit, then give him the "Okay" to let him know that this is the end of the lesson. Praise him so that he knows he did a good job.

The cure for excessive pulling (a common problem) is to stop when the dog is no more than 2 or 3 feet ahead of you. Guide him back into position and begin again. With a really determined puller, try switching to a head collar. This will automatically turn the pup's head toward you so you can bring him back easily to the heel position. Give quiet, reassuring praise every time the leash goes slack and he's staying with you.

Staying and heeling can take a lot out of a dog, so provide playtime and free-running

NO MORE TREATS!

When your dog is responding promptly and correctly to commands, it's time to eliminate treats. Begin by alternating a treat reward with a verbal-praise-only reward. Gradually eliminate all treats while increasing the frequency of praise. Overlook pleading eyes and expectant expressions, but if he's still watching your treat hand, you're on your way to using hand signals.

exercise to shake off the stress when the lessons are over. You don't want him to associate training with all work and no fun.

OBEDIENCE CLASSES

The advantages of an obedience class are that your dog will have to learn amid the distractions of other people and dogs and that your mistakes will be quickly corrected by the trainer. Teaching your dog along with a qualified instructor and other handlers who may have more dog experience than you is another plus of the class environment. The instructor and other handlers can help you to find the most efficient way of teaching your dog a command or exercise. It's often easier to learn by other people's mistakes than your own. You will also learn all of the requirements for competitive obedience trials, in which you can earn titles and go on to advanced jumping and retrieving exercises, which are fun for many dogs. Obedience classes build the foundation needed for many other canine activities (in which we humans are allowed to participate, too!).

TRAINING FOR OTHER ACTIVITIES

Once your dog has basic obedience under his collar and is 12 months of age, you can enter the world of agility training. Dogs think agility is pure fun, like being turned loose in an amusement park full of obstacles! Although not fully recognized by the AKC, the Cesky is eligible to compete in AKC obedience, agility, earthdog and tracking events. For those who like to volunteer, there is the wonderful feeling of owning a therapy dog and visiting hospices, nursing homes and veterans' homes to bring smiles, comfort and companionship to those who live there.

Around the house, your Cesky Terrier can be taught to do some simple chores. You might teach him to carry a basket of household items or to fetch the morning newspaper. The kids can teach the dog all kinds of tricks, from playing hide-and-seek to balancing a biscuit on his nose. A family dog is what rounds out the family. Everything he does beyond sitting in your lap or gazing lovingly at you represents the bonus of owning a dog.

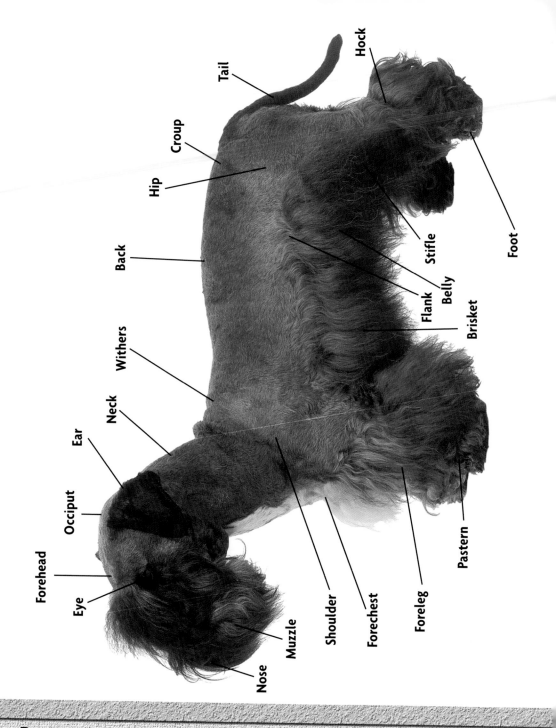

PHYSICAL STRUCTURE OF THE CESKY TERRIER

Hock

Tail

Croup

Hip

Back

Withers

Neck

Ear

Occiput

Forehead

Eye

Nose

Muzzle

Shoulder

Forechest

Foreleg

Pastern

Brisket

Belly

Flank

Stifle

Foot

HEALTHCARE OF YOUR

CESKY TERRIER

By Lowell Ackerman DVM, DACVD

HEALTHCARE FOR A LIFETIME

When you own a dog, you become his healthcare advocate over his entire lifespan, as well as being the one to shoulder the financial burden of such care. Accordingly, it is worthwhile to focus on prevention rather than treatment, as you and your pet will both be happier.

Of course, the best place to have begun your program of preventive healthcare is with the initial purchase or adoption of your dog. There is no way of guaranteeing that your new furry friend is free of medical problems, but there are some things you can do to improve your odds. You certainly should have done adequate research into the Cesky Terrier and have selected your puppy carefully rather than buying on impulse. Health issues aside, a large number of pet abandonment and relinquishment cases arise from a mismatch between pet needs and owner expectations. This is entirely preventable with appropriate planning and finding a good breeder.

Regarding healthcare issues specifically, it is very difficult to make blanket statements about where to acquire a problem-free pet, but, again, a reputable breeder is your best bet. In an ideal situation you have the opportunity to see both parents, get references from other owners of the breeder's pups and see genetic-testing documentation for several generations of the litter's ancestors. At the very least, you must thoroughly investigate your breed of interest and the problems inherent in that breed, as well as the genetic testing available to screen for those problems. Genetic testing offers some important benefits, but testing is available for only a few disorders in a relatively small number of breeds and is not available for some of the most common genetic diseases seen in dogs in general, such as hip dysplasia, cataracts, epilepsy, cardiomyopathy, etc. This area of research is indeed exciting and increasingly important, and advances will continue to be made each year.

1. Esophagus
2. Lungs
3. Spleen
4. Liver
5. Stomach
6. Intestines
7. Urinary Bladder

INTERNAL ORGANS OF THE CESKY TERRIER

We've also discussed that evaluating the behavioral nature of your Cesky Terrier and that of his immediate family members is an important part of the selection process that cannot be underestimated or overemphasized. More dogs are euthanized each year for behavioral reasons than for all medical conditions combined, so it is critical to take temperament issues seriously. Start with a well-balanced, friendly companion and put the time and effort into proper socialization, and you will both be rewarded with a lifelong valued relationship.

Assuming that you have started off with a pup from healthy, sound stock, you then become responsible for helping your veterinarian keep your pet healthy. Some crucial things happen before you even bring your puppy home. Parasite control typically begins at two weeks of age, and vaccinations typically begin at six to eight weeks of age. A pre-pubertal evaluation is typically scheduled for about six months of age. At this time, a dental evaluation is done (since the adult teeth are now in), heartworm prevention is started and neutering or spaying is most commonly done.

It is critical to commence regular dental care at home if you have not already done so. It may not sound very important, but most dogs have active periodontal

TAKING YOUR DOG'S TEMPERATURE

It is important to know how to take your dog's temperature at times when you think he may be ill. It's not the most enjoyable task, but it can be done without too much difficulty. It's easier with a helper, preferably someone with whom the dog is friendly, so that one of you can hold the dog while the other inserts the thermometer.

Before inserting the thermometer, coat the end with petroleum jelly. Insert the thermometer slowly and gently into the dog's rectum about one inch. Wait for the reading, about two minutes. Be sure to remove the thermometer carefully and clean it thoroughly after each use.

A dog's normal body temperature is between 100.5 and 102.5 degrees F. Immediate veterinary attention is required if the dog's temperature is below 99 or above 104 degrees F.

disease by four years of age if they don't have their teeth cleaned regularly at home, not just at their veterinary exams. Dental problems lead to more than just bad "doggie breath." Gum disease can have very serious medical consequences. If you start brushing your dog's teeth and using antiseptic rinses from a young age, your dog will be accustomed to it and will not resist. The results will be healthy

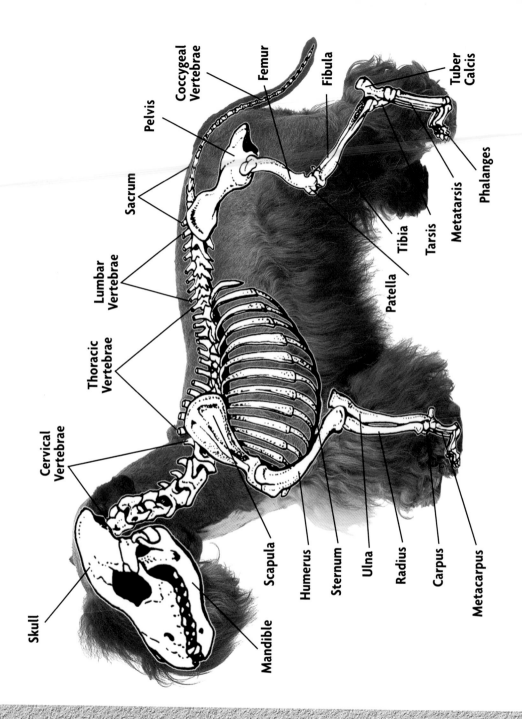

Coccygeal Vertebrae

Femur

Fibula

Tuber Calcis

Pelvis

Phalanges

Sacrum

Tibia

Tarsis

Metatarsis

Lumbar Vertebrae

Thoracic Vertebrae

Patella

Cervical Vertebrae

Skull

Mandible

Scapula

Humerus

Sternum

Ulna

Radius

Carpus

Metacarpus

SKELETAL STRUCTURE OF THE CESKY TERRIER

dentition, which your pet will need to enjoy a long, healthy life.

Most dogs are considered adults at a year of age, although some larger breeds still have some filling out to do up to about two or so years old. Even individual dogs within each breed have different healthcare requirements, so work with your veterinarian to determine what will be needed and what your role should be. This doctor-client relationship is important, because as vaccination guidelines change, there may not be an annual "vaccine visit" scheduled. You must make sure that you see your veterinarian at least annually, even if no vaccines are due, because this is the best opportunity to coordinate health-care activities and to make sure that no medical issues creep by unaddressed.

DOGGIE DENTAL DON'TS

A veterinary dental exam is necessary if you notice one or any combination of the following in your dog:

- Broken, loose or missing teeth
- Loss of appetite (which could be due to mouth pain or illness caused by infection)
- Gum abnormalities, including redness, swelling and bleeding
- Drooling, with or without blood
- Yellowing of the teeth or gumline, indicating tartar
- Bad breath

At the senior stage in your Cesky Terrier's life, your veterinarian may want to schedule visits twice yearly, instead of once, to run some laboratory screenings, electrocardiograms and the like, and to change the diet to something more digestible. Catching problems early is the best way to manage them effectively. Treating the early stages of heart disease is so much easier than trying to intervene when there is more significant damage to the heart muscle. Similarly, managing the beginning of kidney problems is fairly routine if there is no significant kidney damage. Other problems, like cognitive dysfunction (similar to senility and Alzheimer's disease), cancer, diabetes and arthritis, are more common in older dogs, but all can be treated to help the dog live as many happy, comfortable years as possible. Just as in people, medical management is more effective (and less expensive) when you catch things early.

SELECTING A VETERINARIAN

There is probably no more important decision that you will make regarding your pet's health-care than the selection of his doctor. Your pet's veterinarian will be a pediatrician, family-practice physician and gerontologist, depending on the dog's life stage, and will be the individual who makes recommendations regarding issues such as when specialists need to be consulted, when diagnostic testing and/or therapeutic intervention is needed and when you will need to seek outside emergency and critical-care services. Your vet will act as your advocate and liaison throughout these processes.

Everyone has his own idea about what to look for in a vet, an individual who will play a big role in his dog's (and, of course, his own) life for many years to come. For some, it is the compassionate caregiver with whom they hope to develop a professional relationship to span the lifetime of their dogs and even their future pets. For others, they are seeking a clinician with keen diagnostic and therapeutic insight who can deliver state-of-the-art healthcare. Still others need a veterinary facility that is open evenings and weekends, or is in close proximity or provides mobile veterinary

Ah, the joys of a good roll in the grass! Watch what your dog is rolling in, however, as fertilizers and gardening chemicals can be irritating to a dog's skin or even more dangerous.

services, to accommodate their schedules; these people may not much mind that their dogs might see different veterinarians on each visit. Just as we have different reasons for selecting our own healthcare professionals (e.g., covered by insurance plan, expert in field, convenient location, etc.), we should not expect that there is a one-size-fits-all recommendation for selecting a veterinarian and veterinary practice. The best advice is to be honest in your assessment of what you expect from a veterinary practice and to conscientiously research the options in your area. You will quickly appreciate that not all veterinary practices are the same, and you will be happiest with one that truly meets your needs.

There is another point to be considered in the selection of veterinary services. Not that long ago, a single veterinarian would attempt to manage all medical and surgical issues as they arose. That was often problematic, because veterinarians are trained in many species and many diseases, and it was just impossible for general veterinary practitioners to be experts in every species, every field and every ailment. However, just as in the human healthcare fields, specialization has allowed general practitioners to concentrate on primary healthcare delivery, especially wellness and the prevention of infectious diseases, and to utilize a network of specialists to assist in the management of conditions that require specific expertise and experience. Thus there are now many types of veterinary specialists, including dermatologists, cardiologists, ophthalmologists, surgeons, internists, oncologists, neurologists, behaviorists, criticalists and others to help primary-care veterinarians deal with complicated medical challenges. In most cases, specialists see cases referred by primary-care veterinarians, make diagnoses and set up management plans. From there, the animals' ongoing care is returned to their primary-care veterinarians. This important team approach to your pet's medical-care needs has provided opportunities for advanced care and an unparalleled level of quality to be delivered.

With all of the opportunities for your Cesky Terrier to receive high-quality veterinary medical care, there is another topic that needs to be addressed at the same time—cost. It's been said that you can have excellent healthcare or inexpensive healthcare, but never both; this is as true in veterinary medicine as it is in human medicine. While veterinary costs are a fraction of what the same services cost in the human health-care arena, it is still difficult to deal with unanticipated medical costs, especially since they can easily creep into hundreds or even thousands of dollars if specialists or emergency services become involved. However, there are ways of managing these risks. The easiest is to buy pet health insurance and realize that its foremost purpose is not to cover routine healthcare visits but rather to serve as an umbrella for those rainy days when your pet needs medical care and you don't want to worry about whether or not you can afford that care.

Pet insurance policies are very cost-effective (and very inexpensive by human health-insurance standards), but make sure that you buy the policy long before you intend to use it (preferably starting in puppyhood, because coverage will exclude pre-existing conditions) and that you are actually buying an indemnity insurance plan from an insurance company that is regulated by your state or province. Many insurance policy look-alikes are actually discount clubs that are redeemable only at specific locations and for specific services. An indemnity plan covers your pet at almost all veterinary, specialty and emergency practices and is an excellent way to manage your pet's ongoing healthcare needs.

VACCINATIONS AND INFECTIOUS DISEASES

There has never been an easier time to prevent a variety of

COMMON INFECTIOUS DISEASES

Let's discuss some of the diseases that create the need for vaccination in the first place. Following are the major canine infectious diseases and a simple explanation of each.

Rabies: A devastating viral disease that can be fatal in dogs and people. In fact, vaccination of dogs and cats is an important public-health measure to create a resistant animal buffer population to protect people from contracting the disease. Vaccination schedules are determined on a government level and are not optional for pet owners; rabies vaccination is required by law in all 50 states.

Parvovirus: A severe, potentially life-threatening disease that is easily transmitted between dogs. There are four strains of the virus, but it is believed that there is significant "cross-protection" between strains that may be included in individual vaccines.

Distemper: A potentially severe and life-threatening disease with a relatively high risk of exposure, especially in certain regions. In very high-risk distemper environments, young pups may be vaccinated with human measles vaccine, a related virus that offers cross-protection when administered at four to ten weeks of age.

Hepatitis: Caused by canine adenovirus type 1 (CAV-1), but since vaccination with the causative virus has a higher rate of adverse effects, cross-protection is derived from the use of adenovirus type 2 (CAV-2), a cause of respiratory disease and one of the potential causes of canine cough. Vaccination with CAV-2 provides long-term immunity against hepatitis, but relatively less protection against respiratory infection.

Canine cough: Also called tracheobronchitis, actually a fairly complicated result of viral and bacterial offenders; therefore, even with vaccination, protection is incomplete. Wherever dogs congregate, canine cough will likely be spread among them. Intranasal vaccination with *Bordetella* and parainfluenza is the best safeguard, but the duration of immunity does not appear to be very long, typically a year at most. These are non-core vaccines, but vaccination is sometimes mandated by boarding kennels, obedience classes, dog shows and other places where dogs congregate to try to minimize spread of infection.

Leptospirosis: A potentially fatal disease that is more common in some geographic regions. It is capable of being spread to humans. The disease varies with the individual "serovar," or strain, of *Leptospira* involved. Since there does not appear to be much cross-protection between serovars, protection is only as good as the likelihood that the serovar in the vaccine is the same as the one in the pet's local environment. Problems with *Leptospira* vaccines are that protection does not last very long, side effects are not uncommon and a large percentage of dogs (perhaps 30%) may not respond to vaccination.

Borrelia burgdorferi: The cause of Lyme disease, the risk of which varies with the geographic area in which the pet lives and travels. Lyme disease is spread by deer ticks in the eastern US and western black-legged ticks in the western part of the country, and the risk of exposure is high in some regions. Lameness, fever and inappetence are most commonly seen in affected dogs. The extent of protection from the vaccine has not been conclusively demonstrated.

Coronavirus: This disease has a high risk of exposure, especially in areas where dogs congregate, but it typically causes only mild to moderate digestive upset (diarrhea, vomiting, etc.). Vaccines are available, but the duration of protection is believed to be relatively short and the effectiveness of the vaccine in preventing infection is considered low.

There are many other vaccinations available, including those for *Giardia* and canine adenovirus-1. While there may be some specific indications for their use, and local risk factors to be considered, they are not widely recommended for most dogs.

infectious diseases in your dog, but the advances we've made in veterinary medicine come with a price—choice. Now while it may seem that choice is a good thing (and it is), it has never been more difficult for the pet owner (or the veterinarian) to make an informed decision about the best way to protect pets through vaccination.

Years ago, it was just accepted that puppies got a starter series of vaccinations and then annual "boosters" throughout their lives to keep them protected. As more and more vaccines became available, consumers wanted the convenience of having all of that protection in a single injection. The result was "multivalent" vaccines that crammed a lot of protection into a single syringe. The manufacturers' recommendations were to give the vaccines annually, and this was a simple enough protocol to follow. However, as veterinary medicine has become more sophisticated and we have started looking more at healthcare quandaries rather than convenience, it became necessary to reevaluate the situation and deal with some tough questions. It is important to realize that whether or not to use a particular vaccine depends on the risk of contracting the disease against which it protects, the severity of the disease if it is contracted, the duration of immunity provided by the

vaccine, the safety of the product and the needs of the individual animal. In a very general sense, rabies, distemper, hepatitis and parvovirus are considered core vaccine needs, while parainfluenza, *Bordetella bronchiseptica*, leptospirosis, coronavirus and borreliosis (Lyme disease) are considered non-core needs and

PROBLEM: AND THAT STARTS WITH "P"

Urinary tract problems more commonly affect female dogs, especially those who have been spayed. The first sign that a urinary tract problem exists usually is a strong odor from the urine or an unusual color. Blood in the urine, known as hematuria, is another sign of an infection, related to cystitis, a bladder infection, bladder cancer or a blood-clotting disorder. Urinary tract problems can also be signaled by the dog's straining while urinating, experiencing pain during urination and genital discharge as well as excessive water intake and urination.

Excessive drinking, in and of itself, does not indicate a urinary tract problem. A dog who is drinking more than normal may have a kidney or liver problem, a hormonal disorder or diabetes mellitus. Behaviorists report a disorder known as psychogenic polydipsia, which manifests itself in excessive drinking and urination. If you notice your dog drinking much more than normal, take him to the vet.

Puppies love to stop and smell the flowers, but be aware that pollen allergies can affect dogs, too.

aggressive behaviors toward other dogs, and some diminishing of urine marking, roaming and mounting.

While neutering and spaying do indeed prevent animals from contributing to pet overpopulation, even no-cost and low-cost neutering options have not eliminated the problem. Perhaps one of the main reasons for this is that individuals who intentionally breed their dogs and those who allow their animals to run at large are the main causes of unwanted offspring. Also, animals in shelters are often there because they were abandoned or relinquished, not because they came from unplanned matings. Neutering/spaying is important, but it should be considered in the context of the real causes of animals' ending up in shelters and eventually being euthanized.

One of the important considerations regarding neutering is that it is a surgical procedure. This sometimes gets lost in discussions of low-cost procedures and commoditization of the process. In females, spaying is specifically referred to as an ovariohysterectomy. In this procedure, a midline incision is made in the abdomen and the entire uterus and both ovaries are surgically removed. While this is a major invasive surgical procedure, it usually has few

best reserved for animals that demonstrate reasonable risk of contracting the diseases.

NEUTERING/SPAYING

Sterilization procedures (neutering for males/spaying for females) are meant to accomplish several purposes. While the underlying premise is to address the risk of pet overpopulation, there are also some medical and behavioral benefits to the surgeries as well. For females, spaying prior to the first estrus (heat cycle) leads to a marked reduction in the risk of mammary cancer. There also will be no manifestations of "heat" to attract male dogs and no bleeding in the house. For males, there is prevention of testicular cancer and a reduction in the risk of prostate problems. In both sexes, there may be some limited reduction in

complications, because it is typically performed on healthy young animals. However, it is major surgery, as any woman who has had a hysterectomy will attest.

In males, neutering has traditionally referred to castration, which involves the surgical removal of both testicles. While still a significant piece of surgery, there is not the abdominal exposure that is required in the female surgery. In addition, there is now a chemical sterilization option, in which a solution is injected into each testicle, leading to atrophy of the sperm-producing cells. This can typically be done under sedation rather than full anesthesia. This is a relatively new approach, and there are no long-term clinical studies yet available.

Neutering/spaying is typically done around six months of age at most veterinary hospitals, although techniques have been pioneered to perform the procedures in animals as young as eight weeks of age. In general, the surgeries on the very young animals are done for the specific reason of sterilizing them before they go to their new homes. This is done in some shelter hospitals for assurance that the animals will definitely not produce any pups. Otherwise, these organizations need to rely on owners to comply with their wishes to have the animals "altered" at a later date, something that does not always happen.

YOUR DOG NEEDS TO VISIT THE VET IF:

- He has ingested a toxin such as antifreeze or a toxic plant; in these cases, administer first aid and call the vet right away
- His teeth are discolored, loose or missing or he has sores or other signs of infection or abnormality in the mouth
- He has been vomiting, has had diarrhea or has been constipated for over 24 hours; call immediately if you notice blood
- He has refused food for over 24 hours
- His eating habits, water intake or toilet habits have noticeably changed; if you have noticed weight gain or weight loss
- He shows symptoms of bloat, which requires immediate attention
- He is salivating excessively
- He has a lump in his throat
- He has a lumps or bumps anywhere on the body
- He is very lethargic
- He appears to be in pain or otherwise has trouble chewing or swallowing
- His skin loses elasticity

Of course, there will be other instances in which a visit to the vet is necessary; these are just some of the signs that could be indicative of serious problems that need to be caught as early as possible.

S. E. M. BY DR. DENNIS KUNKEL, UNIVERSITY OF HAWAII

A scanning electron micrograph of a dog flea, Ctenocephalides canis, on dog hair.

EXTERNAL PARASITES

FLEAS

Fleas have been around for millions of years and, while we have better tools now for controlling them than at any time in the past, there still is little chance that they will end up on an endangered species list. Actually, they are very well adapted to living on our pets, and they continue to adapt as we make advances.

The female flea can consume 15 times her weight in blood during active reproduction and can lay as many as 40 eggs a day. These eggs are very resistant to the effects of insecticides. They hatch into larvae, which then mature and spin cocoons. The immature fleas reside in this pupal stage until the time is right for feeding. This pupal stage is also very resistant to the effects of insecticides, and pupae can last in the environment without feeding for many months. Newly emergent fleas are attracted to animals by the warmth of the animals' bodies, movement and exhaled carbon dioxide. However, when they first emerge from their cocoons, they orient towards light; thus when an animal passes between a flea and the light source, casting a shadow, the flea pounces and starts to feed. If the animal turns out to be a dog or cat, the reproductive cycle continues. If the flea lands on another type of animal, including a person, the flea will bite but will then look for a more appropriate host. An emerging adult flea can survive without feeding for up to 12 months but, once it tastes blood, it can survive off its host for only three to four days.

It was once thought that fleas spend most of their lives in the environment, but we now know that fleas won't willingly jump off a dog unless leaping to another dog or when physically removed by brushing, bathing or other manipulation. Flea eggs, on the other hand, are shiny and smooth, and they roll off the animal and into the environment. The eggs, larvae and pupae then exist in the environment, but once the adult finds a susceptible animal, it's home sweet home until the flea is forced to seek refuge elsewhere.

Since adult fleas live on the animal and immature forms survive in the environment, a successful treatment plan must address all stages of the flea life cycle. There are now several safe and effective flea-control products that can be applied on a monthly

FLEA PREVENTION FOR YOUR DOG

- Discuss with your veterinarian the safest product to protect your dog, likely in the form of a monthly tablet or a liquid preparation placed on the back of the dog's neck.
- For dogs suffering from flea-bite dermatitis, a shampoo or topical insecticide treatment is required.
- Your lawn and property should be sprayed with an insecticide designed to kill fleas and ticks that lurk outdoors.
- Using a flea comb, check the dog's coat regularly for any signs of parasites.
- Practice good housekeeping. Vacuum floors, carpets and furniture regularly, especially in the areas that the dog frequents, and wash the dog's bedding weekly.
- Follow up house-cleaning with carpet shampoos and sprays to rid the house of fleas at all stages of development. Insect growth regulators are the safest option.

basis. These include fipronil, imidacloprid, selamectin and permethrin (found in several formulations). Most of these products have significant flea-killing rates within 24 hours. However, none of them will control the immature forms in the environment. To accomplish this, there are a variety of insect growth regulators that can be

THE FLEA'S LIFE CYCLE

What came first, the flea or the egg? This age-old mystery is more difficult to comprehend than the

actual cycle of the flea. Fleas usually live only about four months. A female can lay 2,000 eggs in her lifetime.

Egg

Larva

After ten days of rolling around your carpet or under your furniture, the eggs hatch into larvae, which feed on various and sundry debris. In days or

Pupa

months, depending on the climate, the larvae spin cocoons and develop into the pupal or nymph stage, which quickly develop into fleas.

These immature fleas must locate a host within 10 to 14 days or they will die. Only about 1% of the flea population exist as adult fleas, while the other 99% exist as eggs, larvae or pupae.

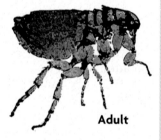

Adult

PHOTO BY CAROLINA BIOLOGICAL SUPPLY CO.

KILL FLEAS THE NATURAL WAY

If you choose not to go the route of conventional medication, there are some natural ways to ward off fleas:

• Dust your dog with a natural flea powder, composed of such herbal goodies as rosemary, wormwood, pennyroyal, citronella, rue, tobacco powder and eucalyptus.

• Apply diatomaceous earth, the fossilized remains of single-cell algae, to your carpets, furniture and pet's bedding. Even though it's not good for dogs, it's even worse for fleas, which will dry up swiftly and die.

• Brush your dog frequently, give him adequate exercise and let him fast occasionally. All of these activities strengthen the dog's system and make him more resistant to disease and parasites.

• Bathe your dog with a capful of pennyroyal or eucalyptus oil.

• Feed a natural diet, free of additives and preservatives. Add some fresh garlic and brewer's yeast to the dog's morning portion, as these items have flea-repelling properties.

sprayed into the environment (e.g., pyriproxyfen, methoprene, fenoxycarb) as well as insect development inhibitors such as lufenuron that can be administered. These compounds have no effect on adult fleas, but they stop immature forms from developing

into adults. In years gone by, we relied heavily on toxic insecticides (such as organophosphates, organochlorines and carbamates) to manage the flea problem, but today's options are not only much safer to use on our pets but also safer for the environment.

TICKS

Ticks are members of the spider class (arachnids) and are blood-sucking parasites capable of transmitting a variety of diseases, including Lyme disease, ehrlichiosis, babesiosis and Rocky Mountain spotted fever. It's easy to see ticks on your own skin, but it is more of a challenge when your Cesky Terrier is affected. Whenever you happen to be planning a stroll in a tick-infested area (especially forests, grassy or wooded areas or parks) be prepared to do a thorough inspection of your dog afterward to search for ticks. Ticks can be tricky, so make sure you spend time looking in the ears, between the toes and everywhere else where a tick might hide. Ticks need to be attached for 24–72 hours before they transmit most of the diseases that they carry, so you do have a window of opportunity for some preventive intervention.

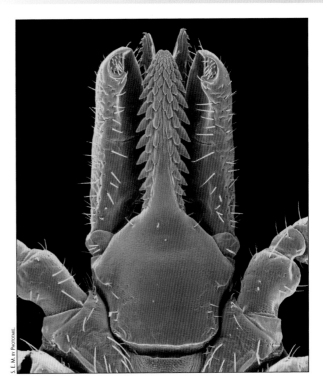

S. E. M. BY PHOTOTAKE.

A scanning electron micrograph of the head of a female deer tick, *Ixodes dammini*, a parasitic tick that carries Lyme disease.

A TICKING BOMB

There is nothing good about a tick's harpooning his nose into your dog's skin. Among the diseases caused by ticks are Rocky Mountain spotted fever, canine ehrlichiosis, canine babesiosis, canine hepatozoonosis and Lyme disease. If a dog is allergic to the saliva of a female wood tick, he can develop tick paralysis.

Female ticks live to eat and breed. They can lay between 4,000 and 5,000 eggs and they die soon after. Males, on the other hand, live only to mate with the females and continue the process as long as they are able. Most ticks live on multiple hosts before parasitizing dogs. The immature forms typically reside on grass and shrubs, waiting for suscep-tible animals to walk by. The larvae and nymph stages typically feed on wildlife.

If only a few ticks are present on a dog, they can be plucked out, but it is important to remove the entire head and mouthparts,

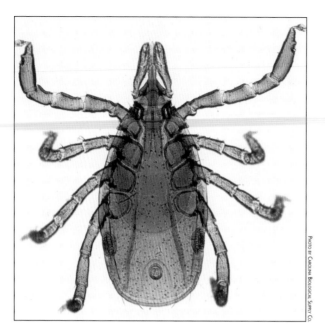

PHOTO BY CAROLINA BIOLOGICAL SUPPLY CO.

Deer tick,
Ixodes dammini.

disposed of in a container of alcohol or household bleach.

Some of the newer flea products, specifically those with fipronil, selamectin and permethrin, have effect against some, but not all, species of tick. Flea collars containing appropriate pesticides (e.g., propoxur, chlorfenvinphos) can aid in tick control. In most areas, such collars should be placed on animals in March, at the beginning of the tick season, and changed regularly. Leaving the collar on when the pesticide level is waning invites the development of resistance. Amitraz collars are also good for tick control, and the active ingredient does not interfere with other flea-control products. The ingredient helps prevent the attachment of ticks to the skin and will cause those ticks already on the skin to detach themselves.

which may be deeply embedded in the skin. This is best accomplished with forceps designed especially for this purpose; fingers can be used but should be protected with rubber gloves, plastic wrap or at least a paper towel. The tick should be grasped as closely as possible to the animal's skin and should be pulled upward with steady, even pressure. Do not squeeze, crush or puncture the body of the tick or you risk exposure to any disease carried by that tick. Once the ticks have been removed, the sites of attachment should be disinfected. Your hands should then be washed with soap and water to further minimize risk of contagion. The tick should be

TICK CONTROL
Removal of underbrush and leaf litter and the thinning of trees in areas where tick control is desired are recommended. These actions remove the cover and food sources for small animals that serve as hosts for ticks. With continued mowing of grasses in these areas, the probability of ticks' surviving is further reduced. A variety of insecticide ingredients (e.g., resmethrin, carbaryl, permethrin, chlorpyrifos, dioxathion and allethrin) are registered for tick control around the home.

MITES

Mites are tiny arachnid parasites that parasitize the skin of dogs. Skin diseases caused by mites are referred to as "mange," and there are many different forms seen in dogs. These forms are very different from one another, each one warranting an individual description.

Sarcoptic mange, or scabies, is one of the itchiest conditions that affects dogs. The microscopic *Sarcoptes* mites burrow into the superficial layers of the skin and can drive dogs crazy with itchiness. They are also communicable to people, although they can't complete their reproductive cycle on people. In addition to being tiny, the mites also are often difficult to find when trying to make a diagnosis. Skin scrapings from multiple areas are examined microscopically but, even then, sometimes the mites cannot be found.

Fortunately, scabies is relatively easy to treat, and there are a variety of products that will successfully kill the mites. Since the mites can't live in the environment for very long without feeding, a complete cure is usually possible within four to eight weeks.

Cheyletiellosis is caused by a relatively large mite, which sometimes can be seen even without a microscope. Often referred to as "walking dandruff," this also causes itching, but not usually as profound as with scabies. While *Cheyletiella* mites can

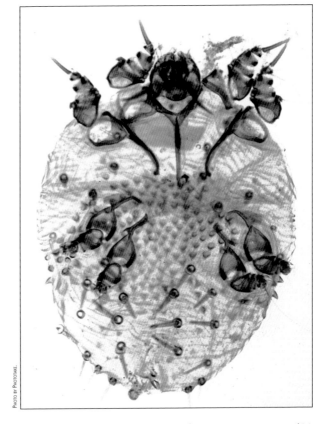

PHOTO BY PHOTOTAKE.

Sarcoptes scabiei, commonly known as the "itch mite."

survive somewhat longer in the environment than scabies mites, they too are relatively easy to treat, being responsive to not only the medications used to treat scabies but also often to flea-control products.

Otodectes cynotis is the canine ear mite and is one of the more common causes of mange, especially in young dogs in shelters or pet stores. That's because the mites are typically present in large numbers and are quickly spread to nearby animals. The mites rarely do

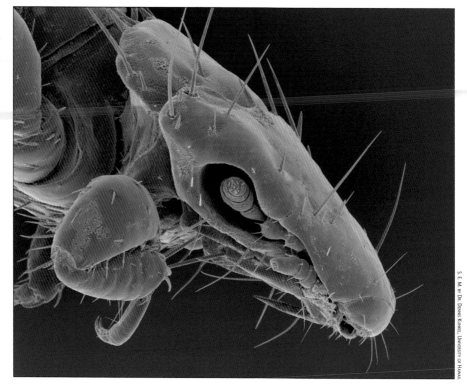

Micrograph of a dog louse, *Heterodoxus spiniger*. Female lice attach their eggs to the hairs of the dog. As the eggs hatch, the larval lice bite and feed on the blood. Lice can also feed on dead skin and hair. This feeding activity can cause hair loss and skin problems.

S. E. M. by Dr. Dennis Kunkel, University of Hawaii.

much harm but can be difficult to eradicate if the treatment regimen is not comprehensive. While many try to treat the condition with ear drops only, this is the most common cause of treatment failure. Ear drops cause the mites to simply move out of the ears and as far away as possible (usually to the base of the tail) until the insecticide levels in the ears drop to an acceptable level—then it's back to business as usual! The successful treatment of ear mites requires treating all animals in the household with a systemic insecticide, such as selamectin, or a combination of miticidal ear drops combined with whole-body flea-control preparations.

Demodicosis, sometimes referred to as red mange, can be one of the most difficult forms of mange to treat. Part of the problem has to do with the fact that the mites live in the hair follicles and they are relatively well shielded from topical and systemic products. The main issue, however, is that demodectic mange typically results only when there is some underlying process interfering with the dog's immune system.

Since *Demodex* mites are normal residents of the skin of

mammals, including humans, there is usually a mite population explosion only when the immune system fails to keep the number of mites in check. In young animals, the immune deficit may be transient or may reflect an actual inherited immune problem. In older animals, demodicosis is usually seen only when there is another disease hampering the immune system, such as diabetes, cancer, thyroid problems or the use of immune-suppressing drugs. Accordingly, treatment involves not only trying to kill the mange mites but also discerning what is interfering with immune function and correcting it if possible.

Chiggers represent several different species of mite that don't parasitize dogs specifically, but do latch on to passersby and can cause irritation. The problem is most prevalent in wooded areas in the late summer and fall. Treatment is not difficult, as the mites do not complete their life cycle on dogs and are susceptible to a variety of miticidal products.

Illustration of Demodex folliculoram.

ILLUSTRATION BY PHOTOTAKE

MOSQUITOES

Mosquitoes have long been known to transmit a variety of diseases to people, as well as just being biting pests during warm weather. They also pose a real risk to pets. Not only do they carry deadly heartworms but recently there also has been much concern over their involvement with West Nile virus. While we can avoid heartworm with the use of preventive medications, there are no such preventives for West Nile virus. The only method of prevention in endemic areas is active mosquito control. Fortunately, most dogs that have been exposed to the virus only developed flu-like symptoms and, to date, there have not been the large number of reported deaths in canines as seen in some other species.

MOSQUITO REPELLENT

Low concentrations of DEET (less than 10%), found in many human mosquito repellents, have been safely used in dogs but, in these concentrations, probably give only about two hours of protection. DEET may be safe in these small concentrations, but since it is not licensed for use on dogs, there is no research proving its safety for dogs. Products containing permethrin give the longest-lasting protection, perhaps two to four weeks. As DEET is not licensed for use on dogs, and both DEET and permethrin can be quite toxic to cats, appropriate care should be exercised. Other products, such as those containing oil of citronella, also have some mosquito-repellent activity, but typically have a relatively short duration of action.

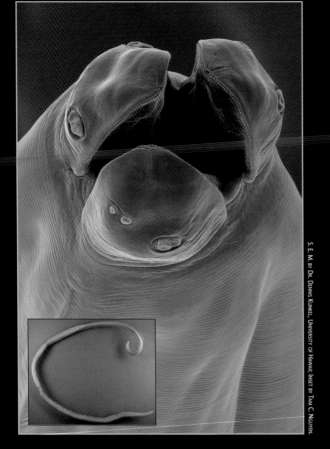

S. E. M. BY DR. DENNIS KUNKEL, UNIVERSITY OF HAWAII; INSET BY TAM C. NGUYEN.

The ascarid roundworm *Toxocara canis,* showing the mouth with three lips. INSET: Photomicrograph of the roundworm *Ascaris lumbricoides.*

INTERNAL PARASITES: WORMS

ASCARIDS

Ascarids are intestinal roundworms that rarely cause severe disease in dogs. Nonetheless, they are of major public health significance because they can be transferred to people. Sadly, it is children who are most commonly affected by the parasite, probably from inadvertently ingesting ascarid-contaminated soil. In fact, many yards and children's sandboxes contain appreciable numbers of ascarid eggs. So, while ascarids don't bite dogs or latch onto their intestines to suck blood, they do cause some nasty medical conditions in children and are best eradicated from our furry friends. Because pups can start passing ascarid eggs by three weeks of age, most parasite-control programs begin at two weeks of age and are repeated every two weeks until pups are eight weeks old. It is important to

S. E. M. BY DR. DENNIS KUNKEL, UNIVERSITY OF HAWAII.

realize that bitches can pass ascarids to their pups even if they test negative prior to whelping. Accordingly, bitches are best treated at the same time as the pups.

HOOKWORMS

Unlike ascarids, hookworms do latch onto a dog's intestinal tract and can cause significant loss of blood and protein. Similar to ascarids, hookworms can be transmitted to humans, where they cause a condition known as cutaneous larval migrans. Dogs can become infected either by consuming the infective larvae or by the larvae's penetrating the skin directly. People most often get infected when they are lying on the ground (such as on a beach) and the larvae penetrate the skin. Yes, the larvae can penetrate through a beach blanket. Hookworms are typically susceptible to the same medications used to treat ascarids.

The hookworm *Ancylostoma caninum* infests the intestines of dogs. INSET: Note the row of hooks at the posterior end, used to anchor the worm to the intestinal wall.

WHIPWORMS

Whipworms latch onto the lower aspects of the dog's colon and can cause cramping and diarrhea. Eggs do not start to appear in the dog's feces until about three months after the dog was infected. This worm has a peculiar life cycle, which makes it more difficult to control than ascarids or hookworms. The good thing is that whipworms rarely are transferred to people.

Some of the medications used to treat ascarids and hookworms are also effective against whipworms, but, in general, a separate treatment protocol is needed. Since most of the medications are effective against the adults but not the eggs or larvae, treatment is typically repeated in three weeks, and then often in three

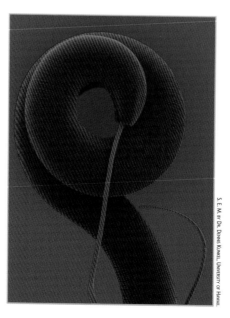

Adult whipworm, *Trichuris* sp., an intestinal parasite.

S. E. M. BY DR. DENNIS KUNKEL, UNIVERSITY OF HAWAII

WORM-CONTROL GUIDELINES

- Practice sanitary habits with your dog and home.
- Clean up after your dog and don't let him sniff or eat other dogs' droppings.
- Control insects and fleas in the dog's environment. Fleas, lice, cockroaches, beetles, mice and rats can act as hosts for various worms.
- Prevent dogs from eating uncooked meat, raw poultry and dead animals.
- Keep dogs and children from playing in sand and soil.
- Kennel dogs on cement or gravel; avoid dirt runs.
- Administer heartworm preventives regularly.
- Have your vet examine your dog's stools at your annual visits.
- Select a boarding kennel carefully so as to avoid contamination from other dogs or an unsanitary environment.
- Prevent dogs from roaming. Obey local leash laws.

---

months as well. Unfortunately, since dogs don't develop resistance to whipworms, it is difficult to prevent them from getting reinfected if they visit soil contaminated with whipworm eggs.

TAPEWORMS

There are many different species of tapeworm that affect dogs, but *Dipylidium caninum* is probably the most common and is spread by fleas. Flea larvae feed on organic debris and tapeworm eggs in the environment and, when a dog chews at himself and manages to ingest fleas, he might get a dose of tapeworm at the same time. The tapeworm then develops further in the intestine of the dog.

The tapeworm itself, which is a parasitic flatworm that latches onto the intestinal wall, is composed of numerous segments. When the segments break off into the intestine (as proglottids), they may accumulate around the rectum, like grains of rice. While this tapeworm is disgusting in its behavior, it is not directly communicable to humans (although humans can also get infected by swallowing fleas).

A much more dangerous flatworm is *Echinococcus multilocularis*, which is typically found in foxes, coyotes and wolves. The eggs are passed in the feces and infect rodents, and, when dogs eat the rodents, the dogs can be infected by thousands of adult tapeworms. While the parasites don't cause many problems in dogs, this is considered the most lethal worm infection that people can get. Take appropriate precautions if you live in an area in which these tapeworms are found. Do not use mulch that may contain feces of dogs, cats or wildlife, and discourage your pets from hunting

wildlife. Treat these tapeworm infections aggressively in pets, because if humans get infected, approximately half die.

HEARTWORMS
Heartworm disease is caused by the parasite *Dirofilaria immitis* and is seen in dogs around the world. A member of the roundworm group, it is spread between dogs by the bite of an infected mosquito. The mosquito injects infective larvae into the dog's skin with its bite, and these larvae develop under the skin for a period of time before making their way to the heart. There they develop into adults, which grow and create blockages of the heart, lungs and major blood vessels there. They also start producing offspring (microfilariae)

A dog tapeworm proglottid (body segment).

The dog tapeworm *Taenia pisiformis*.

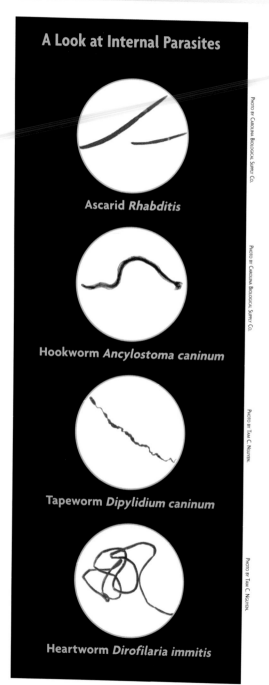

A Look at Internal Parasites

Ascarid *Rhabditis*

PHOTO BY CAROLINA BIOLOGICAL SUPPLY CO.

Hookworm *Ancylostoma caninum*

PHOTO BY CAROLINA BIOLOGICAL SUPPLY CO.

Tapeworm *Dipylidium caninum*

PHOTO BY TAM C. NGUYEN

Heartworm *Dirofilaria immitis*

PHOTO BY TAM C. NGUYEN

and these microfilariae circulate in the bloodstream, waiting to hitch a ride when the next mosquito bites. Once in the mosquito, the microfilariae develop into infective larvae and the entire process is repeated.

When dogs get infected with heartworm, over time they tend to develop symptoms associated with heart disease, such as coughing, exercise intolerance and potentially many other manifestations. Diagnosis is confirmed by either seeing the microfilariae themselves in blood samples or using immunologic tests (antigen testing) to identify the presence of adult heartworms. Since antigen tests measure the presence of adult heartworms and microfilarial tests measure offspring produced by adults, neither are positive until six to seven months after the initial infection. However, the beginning of damage can occur by fifth-stage larvae as early as three months after infection. Thus it is possible for dogs to be harboring problem-causing larvae for up to three months before either type of test would identify an infection.

The good news is that there are great protocols available for preventing heartworm in dogs. Testing is critical in the process, and it is important to understand the benefits as well as the limitations of such testing. All dogs six months of age or older that have not been on continuous heartworm-preventive medication should be

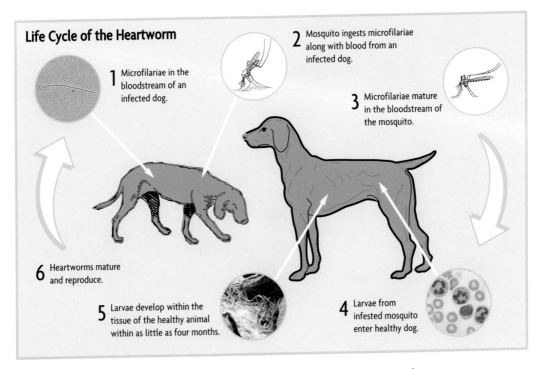

Life Cycle of the Heartworm

1 Microfilariae in the bloodstream of an infected dog.

2 Mosquito ingests microfilariae along with blood from an infected dog.

3 Microfilariae mature in the bloodstream of the mosquito.

4 Larvae from infested mosquito enter healthy dog.

5 Larvae develop within the tissue of the healthy animal within as little as four months.

6 Heartworms mature and reproduce.

screened with microfilarial or antigen tests. For dogs receiving preventive medication, periodic antigen testing helps assess the effectiveness of the preventives. The American Heartworm Society guidelines suggest that annual retesting may not be necessary when owners have absolutely provided continuous heartworm prevention. Retesting on a two- to three-year interval may be sufficient in these cases. However, your veterinarian will likely have specific guidelines under which heartworm preventives will be prescribed, and many prefer to err on the side of safety and retest annually.

It is indeed fortunate that heartworm is relatively easy to prevent, because treatments can be as life-threatening as the disease itself. Treatment requires a two-step process that kills the adult heartworms first and then the microfilariae. Prevention is obviously preferable; this involves a once-monthly oral or topical treatment. The most common oral preventives include ivermectin (not suitable for some breeds), moxidectin and milbemycin oxime; the once-a-month topical drug selamectin provides heartworm protection in addition to flea, tick and other parasite controls.

THE **ABC**s OF
Emergency Care

Abrasions

Clean wound with running water or 3% hydrogen peroxide. Pat dry with gauze and spray with antibiotic. Do not cover.

Animal Bites

Clean area with soap and saline solution or water. Apply pressure to any bleeding area. Apply antibiotic ointment.

Antifreeze Poisoning

Induce vomiting and take dog to the vet.

Bee Sting

Remove stinger and apply soothing lotion or cold compress; give antihistamine in proper dosage.

Bleeding

Apply pressure directly to wound with gauze or towel for five to ten minutes. If wound does not stop bleeding, wrap wound with gauze and adhesive tape.

Bloat/Gastric Torsion

Immediately take the dog to the vet or emergency clinic; phone from car. No time to waste.

Burns

Chemical: Bathe dog with water and pet shampoo. Rinse in saline solution. Apply antibiotic ointment.

Acid: Rinse with water. Apply one part baking soda, two parts water to affected area.

Alkali: Rinse with water. Apply one part vinegar, four parts water to affected area.

Electrical: Apply antibiotic ointment. Seek veterinary assistance immediately.

Choking

If the dog is on the verge of collapsing, wedge a solid object, such as the handle of screwdriver, between molars on one side of the mouth to keep mouth open. Pull tongue out. Use long-nosed pliers or fingers to remove foreign object. Do not push the object down the dog's throat. For small or medium dogs, hold dog upside down by hind legs and shake firmly to dislodge foreign object.

Chlorine Ingestion

With clean water, rinse the mouth and eyes. Give the dog water to drink; contact the vet.

Constipation

Feed dog 2 tablespoons bran flakes with each meal. Encourage drinking water. Mix ¼ teaspoon mineral oil in dog's food.

Diarrhea

Withhold food for 12 to 24 hours. Feed dog antidiarrheal with eyedropper. When feeding resumes, feed one part boiled hamburger, one part plain cooked rice, ¼ to ¾ cup four times daily.

Dog Bite

Snip away hair around puncture wound; clean with 3% hydrogen peroxide; apply tincture of iodine. If wound appears deep, take the dog to the vet.

Frostbite

Wrap the dog in a heavy blanket. Warm affected area with a warm bath for ten minutes. Red color to skin will return with circulation; if tissues are pale after 20 minutes, contact the vet.

Use a portable, durable container large enough to contain all items

Heat Stroke
Submerge the dog in cold water; if no response within ten minutes, contact the vet.

Hot Spots
Mix 2 packets Domeboro® with 2 cups water. Saturate cloth with mixture and apply to hot spots for 15–30 minutes. Apply antibiotic ointment. Repeat every six to eight hours.

Poisonous Plants
Wash affected area with soap and water. Cleanse with alcohol. For foxtail/grass, apply antibiotic ointment.

Rat Poison Ingestion
Induce vomiting. Keep dog calm, maintain dog's normal body temperature (use blanket or heating pad). Get to the vet for antidote.

Shock
Keep the dog calm and warm; call for veterinary assistance.

Snake Bite
If possible, bandage the area and apply pressure. If the area is not conducive to bandaging, use ice to control bleeding. Get immediate help from the vet.

Tick Removal
Apply flea and tick spray directly on tick. Wait one minute. Using tweezers or wearing plastic gloves, grasp the tick's body firmly. Apply antibiotic ointment.

Vomiting
Restrict dog's water intake; offer a few ice cubes. Withhold food for next meal. Contact vet if vomiting persists longer than 24 hours.

DOG OWNER'S FIRST-AID KIT

- ☐ Gauze bandages/swabs
- ☐ Adhesive and non-adhesive bandages
- ☐ Antibiotic powder
- ☐ Antiseptic wash
- ☐ Hydrogen peroxide 3%
- ☐ Antibiotic ointment
- ☐ Lubricating jelly
- ☐ Rectal thermometer
- ☐ Nylon muzzle
- ☐ Scissors and forceps
- ☐ Eyedropper
- ☐ Syringe
- ☐ Anti-bacterial/fungal solution
- ☐ Saline solution
- ☐ Antihistamine
- ☐ Cotton balls
- ☐ Nail clippers
- ☐ Screwdriver/pen knife
- ☐ Flashlight
- ☐ Emergency phone numbers

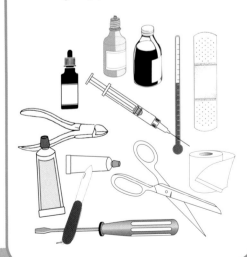

CDS: Cognitive Dysfunction Syndrome

"Old-Dog Syndrome"

There are many ways for you to evaluate old-dog syndrome. Veterinarians have defined CDS (cognitive dysfunction syndrome) as the gradual deterioration of cognitive abilities, indicated by changes in the dog's behavior. When a dog changes his routine response, and maladies have been eliminated as the cause of these behavioral changes, then CDS is the usual diagnosis.

More than half the dogs over eight years old suffer from some form of CDS. The older the dog, the more chance he has of suffering from CDS. In humans, doctors often dismiss the CDS behavioral changes as part of "winding down."

There are four major signs of CDS: frequent potty accidents inside the home, sleeping much more or much less than normal, acting confused and failing to respond to social stimuli.

Symptoms of CDS

FREQUENT POTTY ACCIDENTS
• Urinates in the house.
• Defecates in the house.
• Doesn't signal that he wants to go out.

FAILURE TO RESPOND TO SOCIAL STIMULI
• Comes to people less frequently, whether called or not.
• Doesn't tolerate petting for more than a short time.
• Doesn't come to the door when you return home.

CONFUSION
• Goes outside and just stands there.
• Appears confused with a faraway look in his eyes.
• Hides more often.
• Doesn't recognize friends.
• Doesn't come when called.
• Walks around listlessly and without a destination.

SLEEP PATTERNS
• Awakens more slowly.
• Sleeps more than normal during the day.
• Sleeps less during the night.

CESKY TERRIER

WHEN IS MY DOG A "SENIOR"?

In general, purebred dogs are considered to have achieved senior status when they reach 75% of their breed's average lifespan, with lifespan being based on size and breed-specific health factors. Your Cesky Terrier has an average lifespan of 10–15 years and thus is a senior citizen at around 7 or 8.

Obviously, the old "seven dog years to one human year" theory is not exact. In puppyhood, a dog's year is actually comparable to more than seven human years, considering the puppy's rapid growth during his first year. Then, in adulthood, the ratio decreases. Regardless, the more viable rule of thumb is that the larger the dog, the shorter his expected lifespan. Of course, this can vary among individual dogs, with many living longer than expected, which we hope is the case!

WHAT ARE THE SIGNS OF AGING?

By the time your dog has reached his senior years, you will know him very well, so the physical and behavioral changes that accompany aging should be noticeable to you. Humans and dogs share the most obvious physical sign of aging: gray hair! Graying often occurs first on the

ADAPTING TO AGE

As dogs age and their once-keen senses begin to deteriorate, they can experience stress and confusion. However, dogs are very adaptable, and most can adjust to deficiencies in their sight and hearing. As these processes often deteriorate gradually, the dog makes adjustments gradually, too. Because dogs become so familiar with the layout of their homes and yards, and with their daily routines, they are able to get around even if they cannot see or hear as well. Help your senior dog by keeping things consistent around the house. Keep up with your regular times for walking and potty trips, and do not relocate his crate or rearrange the furniture. Your dog is a very adaptable creature and can make compensation for his diminished ability, but you want to help him along the way and not make changes that will cause him confusion.

Terriers, in general, are hardy dogs who remain keen and alert as they age. This older Cesky certainly doesn't look like a senior!

muzzle and face, around the eyes. Other telltale signs are the dog's overall decrease in activity. Your older dog might be more content to nap and rest, and he may not show the same old enthusiasm when it's time to play in the yard or go for a walk. Other physical signs include significant weight loss or gain; more labored movement; skin and coat problems, possibly hair loss; sight and/or hearing problems; changes in toileting habits, perhaps seeming "unhousebroken" at times; tooth decay, bad breath or other mouth problems.

There are behavioral changes that go along with aging, too. There are numerous causes for behavioral changes. Sometimes a dog's apparent confusion results from a physical change like diminished sight or hearing. If his

confusion causes him to be afraid, he may act aggressively or defensively. He may sleep more frequently because his daily walks, though shorter now, tire him out. He may begin to experience separation anxiety or, conversely, become less interested in petting and attention.

There also are clinical conditions that cause behavioral changes in older dogs. One such condition is known as cognitive dysfunction (familiarly known as "old-dog" syndrome). It can be frustrating for an owner whose dog is affected with cognitive dysfunction, as it can result in behavioral changes of all types, most seemingly unexplainable.

Disease also can be the cause of behavioral changes in senior dogs. Hormonal problems (Cushing's disease is common in older dogs), diabetes and thyroid disease can cause increased appetite, which can lead to aggression related to food guarding. It's better to be proactive with your senior dog, making more frequent trips to the vet if necessary and having bloodwork done to test for the diseases that can commonly befall older dogs.

The aforementioned changes are discussed to alert owners to the things that may happen as their dogs get older. Many hardy dogs remain active and alert well into old age. However, it can be frustrating and heartbreaking for owners to see their beloved dogs change physically and temperamentally. Just know that it's the same Cesky Terrier under there, and that he still loves you and appreciates your care, which he needs now more than ever.

HOW DO I CARE FOR MY AGING DOG?

Again, every dog is an individual in terms of aging. Even if your Cesky shows no outward signs of aging, he should begin a senior-care program once he reaches the determined age. By providing him with extra attention to his veterinary care at this age, you will be practicing good preventive medicine, ensuring that the rest of your dog's life will be as long, active, happy and healthy as possible. If you do notice indications of aging, such as graying and/or changes in sleeping, eating or toileting habits, this is a sign to set up a senior-care visit with your vet right away to make sure that these changes are not related to any health problems.

To start, senior dogs should visit the vet twice yearly for exams, routine tests and overall evaluations. Many veterinarians have special screening programs especially for senior dogs that can include a thorough physical exam; blood test to determine complete blood count; serum biochemistry test, which screens for liver, kidney and blood problems as well as cancer; urinalysis; and dental exams. With these tests, it can be determined whether your dog has any health problems; the results also establish a baseline for your pet against which future test results can be compared.

In addition to these tests, your vet may suggest additional testing, including an EKG, tests for glaucoma and other problems of the eye, chest X-rays, screening for tumors, blood pressure test, test for thyroid function and screening for parasites and reassessment of his preventive program. Your vet also will ask you questions about your dog's diet and activity level, what you feed and the amounts that you feed. This information, along with his evaluation of the dog's overall condition, will enable him to suggest proper dietary changes, if needed.

This may seem like quite a work-up for your pet, but veterinarians advise that older dogs need more frequent attention so that any health problems can be detected as early as possible. Serious conditions like kidney disease, heart disease and cancer may not present outward symptoms, or the problem may go undetected if the symptoms are mistaken by owners as just part of the aging process.

There are some conditions more common in elderly dogs that are difficult to ignore. Cognitive dysfunction shares much in common with senility and Alzheimer's disease, and dogs are not immune. Dogs can become confused and/or disoriented, lose their house-training, have abnormal sleep-wake cycles and interact differently with their owners. Be heartened by the fact that, in some ways, there are more treatment options for dogs with cognitive dysfunction than for people with similar conditions. There is good evidence that continued stimulation in the form of games, play, training and exercise can help to maintain cognitive function. There are also medications (such as seligiline) and antioxidant-fortified senior diets that have been shown to be beneficial.

Cancer is also a condition more common in the elderly. While lung cancer, which is a major killer in humans, is relatively rare in dogs, almost all of the cancers seen in people are also seen in pets. If pets are getting regular physical examinations, cancers are often detected early. There are a variety of cancer therapies available today, and many pets continue to live happy lives with appropriate treatment.

Degenerative joint disease, often referred to as arthritis, is another malady common to both elderly dogs and humans. A lifetime of wear and tear on joints and running around at play eventually take toll and result in

stiffness and difficulty in getting around. As dogs live longer and healthier lives, it is natural that they should eventually feel some of the effects of aging. Once again, if your Cesky has had regular veterinary care throughout his life, he should not have been carrying extra pounds all those years and wearing those joints out before their time. If your pet was unfortunate enough to inherit hip dysplasia, osteochondrosis dissecans, or any of the other developmental orthopedic diseases, battling the onset of degenerative joint disease was probably a longstanding goal. In any case, there are now many effective remedies for managing degenerative joint disease and a number of remarkable surgeries as well.

Aside from the extra veterinary care, there is much you can do at home to keep your older dog in good condition. The dog's diet is an important factor. If your dog's appetite decreases, he will not be getting the nutrients he needs. He also will lose weight, which is unhealthy for a dog at a proper weight. Conversely, an older dog's metabolism is slower and he usually exercises less, but he should not be allowed to become obese. Obesity in an older dog is especially risky, because extra pounds mean extra stress on the body, increasing his vulnerability to heart disease. Additionally, the extra pounds make it harder for the dog to move about.

You should discuss age-related feeding changes with your vet. For a dog who has lost interest in food, it may be suggested to try some different types of food until you find something new that the dog likes. For an obese dog, a "light" formula dog food or reducing food portions may be advised, along with exercise appropriate to his physical condition and energy level.

As for exercise, the senior dog should not be allowed to become a "couch potato" despite his old age. Keep up with your daily walks, but keep the distances shorter and let your dog set the pace. If he gets to the point where he's not up for walks, let him stroll around the yard. On the other hand, many dogs remain very active in their senior years, so base changes to the exercise program on your own individual dog and what he's capable of. Don't worry, your Cesky Terrier will let you know when it's time to rest.

Keep up with your grooming routine as you always have. Be extra diligent about checking the skin and coat for problems. Older dogs can experience thinning coats as a normal aging process, but they can also lose hair as a result of medical problems. Some thinning is normal, but patches of baldness or the loss of significant amounts of hair is not.

Hopefully, you've been regular with brushing your dog's teeth throughout his life. Healthy teeth directly affect overall good health. We already know that bacteria from gum infections can enter the dog's body through the damaged gums and travel to the organs. At a stage in life when his organs don't function as well as they used to, you don't want anything to put additional strain on them. Clean teeth also contribute to a healthy immune system. Offering the dental-type chews in addition to toothbrushing can help, as they remove plaque and tartar as the dog chews.

Along with the same good care you've given him all of his life, pay a little extra attention to your dog in his senior years and keep up with twice-yearly trips to the vet. The sooner a problem is uncovered, the greater the chances of a full recovery.

Your senior Cesky will let you know when it's time for a break! Older dogs especially appreciate soft padded areas on which to rest, as they can develop stiffness or other aches and pains.

"CZECHING OUT" YOUR CESKY

You have found your Cesky puppy and he is endearing himself to your family. He is developing and growing on schedule. Now is the time to reacquaint yourself with the

Hailing from the UK is Amore Amore Talyot.

Cesky standard. How does your pup measure up? Remember, this breed is a go-to-ground earthdog. You should be able to span his chest between your hands. If oversized, he cannot do the work for which he was bred. At one year of age, he should be fully grown, 16–18 pounds preferred.

But wait a minute! All of a sudden, your prospective "show star" is oversized. This precludes him from being shown, so what to do now? Well, there are lots of avenues open to you and your puppy. Good citizen tests, obedience, agility and flyball are but a few suggestions. More outgoing personalities may enjoy therapy work, visiting nursing homes, child development centers and therapy groups for the handicapped. Of course, various clubs offer earthdog trials for your terrier, and the list goes on. Let your imagination run wild and be your guide. Not every dog is a show dog, but all dogs are wonderful and can be successful at endeavors they enjoy. Let's examine conformation showing and some other areas of the dog sport.

BEFORE YOU SHOW

When you purchase your Cesky Terrier, you will make it clear to the breeder whether you want one just as a lovable companion and pet or if you hope to be buying a

Cesky with show prospects. No reputable breeder will sell you a young puppy and tell you that it is *definitely* of show quality, for so much can go wrong during the early months of a puppy's development. If you plan to show, what you will hopefully have acquired is a puppy with "show potential."

To the novice, exhibiting a Cesky Terrier in the show ring may look easy, but it takes a lot of hard work and devotion to do top winning at a national or inter-national show, not to mention a little luck too!

The first concept that the canine novice learns when watching a dog show is that each dog first competes against members of his own breed. Once the judge has selected the best member of each breed (Best of Breed), provided that the show is judged on a group system, that chosen dog will compete with other dogs in his group. Finally, the dogs chosen first in each group will compete for Best in Show.

The second concept that you must understand is that the dogs are not actually compared against one another. The judge compares each dog against his breed standard, the written description of the ideal specimen that is approved by the national kennel club. While some early breed standards were indeed based on specific dogs that were famous or

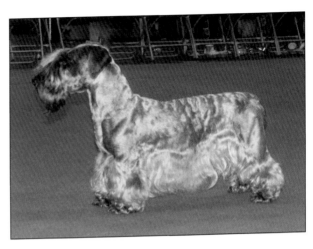

A German representative of the breed, Zeus of Bumble Bee Castle. Owner, Michael Weser.

popular, many dedicated enthusiasts say that a perfect specimen, as described in the standard, has never walked into a show ring, has never been bred and, to the woe of dog breeders around the globe, does not exist. Breeders attempt to get as close to this ideal as possible with every litter, but theoretically the "perfect" dog is so elusive that it is impossible. (And if the "perfect" dog were born, breeders and judges would never agree that it was indeed "perfect.")

If you are interested in exploring the world of dog showing, your best bet is to join your regional breed club, if there is one in your area, or the national parent club (the National Cesky Terrier Club of America). Breed clubs often host both regional and national specialties, shows only for Cesky Terriers, which can include conformation as well as obedience, agility trials and even earthdog events. The breed also is eligible to participate in "B" conformation matches held by the AKC. Even if you have no intention of competing with your Cesky, a specialty is like a festival for lovers of the breed who congregate to share their favorite topic: the Cesky Terrier! Clubs also send out newsletters, and some organize training days and seminars in order that people may learn more about their chosen breed.

If your Cesky Terrier is six months of age or older and registered with the national kennel club, you can enter him a dog show where the breed is offered classes. Provided that your Cesky Terrier does not have a disqualifying fault, he can compete. Only unaltered dogs can be entered in a dog show, so if you have spayed or neutered your Cesky Terrier, you cannot compete in conformation shows. The reason for this is simple. Dog shows are the main forum to prove which representatives in a breed are worthy of being bred. Only dogs that have achieved championships—the dog world's "seal of approval" for excellence in pure-bred dogs—should be bred. Altered dogs, however, can participate in other events such as obedience, agility and "good citizen" certification.

HANDLING BASICS

Before you actually step into the ring, you would be well advised to sit back and observe the judge's ring procedure. If it is your first time in the ring, do not be over-anxious and run to the front of the line. It is much better to stand back and study how the exhibitor in front of you is performing. The judge asks each handler to "stack" the dog, hopefully showing the dog off to his best advantage. The judge will observe the dog from a distance and from different angles, and approach the dog to check his teeth, overall structure, alertness and muscle tone, as well as consider how well the dog "conforms" to the standard. Most importantly, the judge will have the exhibitor move the dog

EXPRESS YOURSELF

The most intangible of all canine attributes, expression speaks to the character of the breed, attained by the combined features of the head. The shape and balance of the dog's skull, the color and position of the eyes and the size and carriage of the head mingle to produce the correct expression of the breed. A judge may approach a dog and determine instantly whether the dog's face portrays the desired impression for the breed, conveying nobility, intelligence and alertness among other specifics of the breed standard.

around the ring in some pattern that he should specify. Finally, the judge will give the dog one last look before moving on to the next exhibitor.

If you are not in the top four in your class at your first show, do not be discouraged. Be patient and consistent, and you may eventually find yourself in a winning line-up. Remember that the winners were once in your shoes and have devoted many hours and much money to earn the placement. If you find that your dog is losing every time and never getting a nod, it may be time to consider a different dog sport or to just enjoy your Cesky Terrier as a pet.

OTHER TYPES OF COMPETITION

In addition to AKC "B" matches, the Cesky Terrier is eligible for participation in AKC performance events as well as, of course, those held by Cesky Terrier and rare-breed clubs. The AKC vote in July 2003 allowed the breed into agility, obedience and tracking, and a November 2003 vote allowed the breed into earthdog events. The breed's eligibility for all of these events became effective on January 1, 2004.

Basic ring procedure includes gaiting the dog at a good pace in line with the other exhibitors, following the pattern specified by the judge.

OBEDIENCE TRIALS

Mrs. Helen Whitehouse Walker, a Standard Poodle fancier, can be credited with introducing obedience trials to the United States. In the 1930s she designed a series of exercises based on those of the Associated Sheep, Police, Army Dog Society of Great Britain. These exercises were intended to evaluate the working relationship between dog and owner. Since those early days of the sport in the US, obedience trials have grown more and more popular, and now more than 2,000 trials each year attract over 100,000 dogs and their owners. Any dog registered with the AKC, regardless of neutering or other disqualifications that would preclude entry in conformation competition, can participate in obedience trials.

There are three levels of difficulty in obedience competition. The first (and easiest) level is the Novice, in which dogs can earn the Companion Dog (CD) title. The intermediate level is the Open level, in which the Companion Dog Excellent (CDX) title is awarded. The advanced level is the Utility level, in which dogs compete for the Utility Dog (UD) title. Classes at each level are further divided into "A" and "B," with "A" for beginners and "B" for those with more experience. In order to win a title at a given level, a dog must earn three

"legs." A "leg" is accomplished when a dog scores 170 or higher (200 is a perfect score). The scoring system gets a little trickier when you understand that a dog must score more than 50% of the points available for each exercise in order to actually earn the points. Available points for each exercise range between 20 and 40.

Once he's earned the UD title, a dog can go on to win the prestigious title of Utility Dog Excellent (UDX) by winning "legs" in ten shows. Additionally, Utility Dogs who win "legs" in Open B and Utility B earn points toward the lofty title of Obedience Trial Champion (OTCh.). Established in 1977 by the AKC, this title requires a dog to earn 100 points as well as three first places in a combination of Open B and Utility B classes under three different judges.

BREED FIRSTS IN THE US

Success is the name of the game for Claire and Kathy Reed of Florida. Three of their Ceskies have earned historical firsts in the US. Casey Alchemy Narration Artist became the first United Kennel Club obedience-titled dog. Windrush Clipper Full Sail became the first American Kennel Club and American Working Terrier Association titled Earthdog. Chalma's Angelica became the first UKC conformation champion. This accomplished trio is owned, trained and handled by the Reeds.

AGILITY TRIALS

Agility trials became sanctioned by the AKC in August 1994, when the first licensed agility trials were held. Since that time, agility certainly has grown in popularity by leaps and bounds, literally! The AKC allows all registered breeds (including Miscellaneous Class breeds) to participate, providing the dog is 12 months of age or older. Agility is designed so that the handler demonstrates how well the dog can work at his side. The handler directs his dog through, over, under and around an obstacle course that includes jumps, tires, the dog walk, weave poles, pipe tunnels, collapsed tunnels and more. While working his way through the course, the dog must keep one eye and ear on the handler and the rest of his body on the course. The handler runs along with the dog, giving verbal and hand signals to guide the dog through the course.

The first organization to promote agility trials in the US was the United States Dog Agility Association, Inc. (USDAA). Established in 1986, the USDAA sparked the formation of many member clubs around the country. To participate in USDAA trials, dogs must be at least 18 months of age. The USDAA and AKC both offer titles to winning dogs, although the exercises and requirements of the two organizations differ.

FOR MORE INFORMATION....

For reliable up-to-date information about registration, dog shows and other canine competitions, contact one of the national registries by mail or via the Internet.

American Kennel Club
5580 Centerview Dr., Raleigh, NC 27606-3390
www.akc.org

United Kennel Club
100 E. Kilgore Road, Kalamazoo, MI 49002
www.ukcdogs.com

Canadian Kennel Club
89 Skyway Ave., Suite 100, Etobicoke, Ontario M9W 6R4 Canada
www.ckc.ca

American Rare Breed Association
9921 Frank Tippett Road
Cheltenham, MD 20623
info@arba.org

Continental Kennel Club
PO Box 1628
Walker, LA 70785
www.ckcusa.org

Agility trials are a great way to keep your dog active, and they will keep you running, too! You should join a local agility club to learn more about the sport. These clubs offer sessions in which you can introduce your dog to the various obstacles as well as training classes to prepare him for competition. In no time, your dog will be climbing A-frames, crossing the dog walk and flying over hurdles, all with you right beside him. Your heart will leap every time your dog jumps through the hoop—and you'll be having just as much (if not more) fun!

TRACKING

Tracking tests are exciting ways to test your Cesky Terrier's instinctive scenting ability on a competitive level. All dogs have a nose, and all breeds are welcome in tracking tests. The first AKC-licensed tracking test took place in 1937 as part of the Utility level at an obedience trial, and thus competitive tracking was officially begun. The first title, Tracking Dog (TD), was offered in 1947, ten years after the first official tracking test. It was not until 1980 that the AKC added the title Tracking Dog Excellent (TDX), which was followed by the title Versatile Surface Tracking (VST) in 1995. Champion Tracker (CT) is awarded to a dog who has earned all three of those titles.

EARTHDOG EVENTS

As the Cesky Terrier historically is a true "go-to-ground" earthdog, the National Cesky Terrier Club of America offers earthdog titles to preserve the breed's innate hunting skills. Although Ceskies in the US are not typically used as working dogs, Cesky owners are encouraged to participate in earthdog events with their dogs. Not only are they fun for dog and owner, but they encourage the earthdog instinct that is so much a part of the Cesky's heritage.

The NCTCA does not run earthdog events itself; rather, the club awards titles to dogs who have competed successfully in an approved club's earthdog events. Owners must provide proper documentation to the NCTCA to prove the dog's accomplishments. For more information, contact the NCTCA, the AKC or the American Working Terrier Association (AWTA).

There are four levels in AKC earthdog trials. The first, Introduction to Quarry, is for beginners and uses a 10-foot tunnel. No title is awarded at this level. The Junior Earthdog (JE) title is awarded at the next level, which uses a 30-foot tunnel with three 90-degree turns. Two qualifying JE runs are required for a dog to earn the title. The next level, Senior Earthdog (SE), uses the same length tunnel and number of turns as in the JE level, but also has a false den and exit and requires the dog to come out of the tunnel when called. To try for the SE title, a dog must have at least his JE; the SE title requires three qualifying runs at this level. The most difficult of the earthdog tests, Master Earthdog (ME), again uses the 30-foot tunnel with three 90-degree turns, with a false entrance, exit and den. The dog is required to enter in the right place as well as honor another working dog. The ME title requires four qualifying runs, and a dog must have earned his SE title to attempt the ME level.

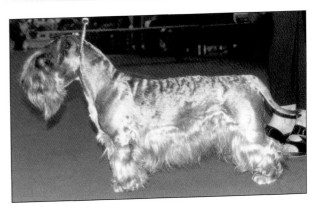

A show dog from Finland, Cantabile Puccini.

A TRIP ABROAD WITH YOUR CESKY

Once the Cesky Terrier has a complete hold of your heart, you will consider becoming a transatlantic fancier. The truly dedicated hard-core fanciers spend their vacation time visiting the Czech Republic. In the first week of May each year, the Czech Cesky Club sponsors a meeting and a show in Melnik. All owners and fanciers are welcome to this all-Cesky event. The casual Cesky owner can meet the world's most famous Cesky breeders, judges and handlers. The event includes demonstrations on how to handle and groom a Cesky as well as a fun working trial, a club show, a wonderful banquet and lots of information sharing. Learn more about the event from the Czech Cesky Club's website at www.volny.cz/kchct.

FÉDÉRATION CYNOLOGIQUE INTERNATIONALE

The Fédération Cynologique Internationale (FCI) aims to encourage and promote the breeding and use of pure-bred dogs that properly represent their breed standards and are capable of working in their bred-for capacities, as well as to protect the breeding and keeping of dogs around the world and to support the open exchange of dogs and information between member countries. Founded on May 22, 1911, the FCI today operates around the world in 79 member countries, divided into five regional groups, which include Europe; the Americas and the Caribbean; Asia; Africa; and Oceania and Australia. When the organization was established it included only five countries: Germany, Austria, France, Netherlands and Belgium. The Société Royale Saint-Hubert of Belgium deserves credit for recreating the organization in 1921 after it disappeared during World War I.

Recognizing over 330 breeds, nearly twice the number of any other registry, the FCI considers each breed as the "property" of its native country and recognizes the breed standard of the country of origin. All 79 member countries conduct both international shows and working/hunting trials. National shows are held, though these shows are governed by the rules of the member country and not the FCI.

FCI conformation shows are sometimes called "beauty shows" and differ in many respects from the shows of other kennel clubs. For example, each dog is critiqued by the judge in writing, and these "judge's reports" are available to the exhibitor. The judge must detail his evaluation and designate a grade to the dog, based entirely on conformation to the standard. This process is far more time-consuming than that of other kennel clubs and also demands that the judge be able to "document" his decision for placing the dog first or last. The judges assign the following qualifications to dogs: Excellent (close to ideal, excellent condition, good balance and superior presentation); Very Good (typical of breed and well-balanced, with a few minor faults); Good (most breed characteristics with faults), Sufficient or Satisfactory (corresponds to breed but not typical), Disqualified (atypical with serious faults) and Cannot Be Judged (uncontrolled in ring).

The FCI's most prestigious shows are the all-breed shows, such as the World Dog Show, followed by the Sections shows, like the European Dog Show, and then the International Championship Shows. National shows can be all-breed shows, Group Championship Shows, Breed or Specialty Shows, Open Shows, Club Shows and Young Dog Shows. At all of these shows, dogs can earn World or European Championship titles or the CACIB certificate. The *Certificat d'Aptitude au Championnat International de Beauté* is the International Certificate won by dogs; the National Certificate is known as the *Certificat d'Aptitude au Championnat National de Beauté* (CAC). The judge awards the CACIB certificate to a superior dog in the Open, Working or Champion Class. A dog that has won four CACIBs (without working or hunting trial) is designated an International Beauty Champion, provided that the certificates were won in three different countries, one of which must be the country of residence or origin. The title National Beauty Champion is awarded to a dog who has earned two, three or four CACs, depending on the country. The titles International Champion and National Champion are reserved only for those breeds that must undergo working or hunting trials.

The following classes are offered at FCI shows: Puppy Class (6–9 months of age), Junior Class (9–18 months of age), Intermediate Class (15–24 months of age), Open Class, Working Class and Champion Class (these latter three, all 15 months of age and over); Veterans Class (eight years of age and over).

For more information about the FCI, show schedules and rules and regulations, you can visit the website at www.fci.be. The FCI also publishes the *Trimestrial Magazine* in four languages (French, English, German and Spanish). Contact Stratego, Muhlenweg 4, 7221 Marz, Austria for information about the magazine.

TEN GROUPS

The FCI is divided into ten groups that classify the breeds by traditional functions. The official breed list indicates whether or not the breed requires a Working Trial in order to earn the CACIB title.

Group 1: Sheepdogs and Cattledogs (except Swiss Cattledogs)

Group 2: Pinschers and Schnauzers, Molossians, Swiss Mountain dogs and Swiss Cattledogs

Group 3: Terriers

Group 4: Dachshunds

Group 5: Spitz- and Primitive-type dogs

Group 6: Scenthounds and related breeds

Group 7: Pointing dogs

Group 8: Retrievers, Flushing dogs and Water dogs

Group 9: Companion and Toy dogs

Group 10: Sighthounds

CESKY TERRIER

UNDERSTANDING THE CANINE MINDSET

For starters, you and your dog are on different wavelengths. Your dog is similar to a toddler in that both live in the present tense only. A dog's view of life is based primarily on cause and effect, which is similar to the old saying, "Nothing teaches a youngster to hang on like falling off the swing." If your dog stumbles down a flight of three steps, the next time he hopefully will walk more carefully or may avoid the steps altogether.

Your dog makes connections based on the fact that he lives in the present, so when he is doing something and you interrupt to dispense praise or a correction, a connection, positive or negative, is made. To the dog, that's like one plus one equals two! In the same sense, it's also easy to see that when your timing is off, you will cause an incorrect connection. The one-plus-one way of thinking is why you must never scold a dog for behavior that took place an hour, 15 minutes or even 5 seconds ago. But it is also why,

when your timing is perfect, you can teach him to do all kinds of wonderful things—as soon as he has made that essential connection. What helps the process is his desire to please you and to have your approval.

There are behaviors we admire in dogs, such as friendliness and obedience, as well as those behaviors that cause problems to a varying degree. The dog owner who encounters minor behavioral problems is wise to solve them promptly or get professional help. Bad behaviors are not corrected by repeatedly shouting "No" or getting angry with the dog. Only the giving of praise and approval for good behavior lets your dog understand right from wrong. The longer a bad behavior is allowed to continue, the harder it is to overcome. A responsible breeder is often able to help. Each dog is unique, so try not to compare your dog's behavior with that of your neighbor's dog or the one you had as a child.

Have your veterinarian check the dog to see whether a behavior problem could have a physical cause. An earache or toothache, for example, could be the reason for a dog to snap at you if you were to touch his head when putting on his leash. A sharp correction from you would only increase the behavior. When a physical basis is eliminated, and if the problem is not something you understand or can cope with, ask for the name of a behavioral specialist, preferably one who is familiar with the Cesky Terrier. Be sure to keep the breeder informed of your progress.

Many things, such as environment and inherited traits, form the basic behavior of a dog, just as in humans. You also must factor into his temperament the purpose for which your dog was originally bred. The major obstacle lies in the dog's inability to explain his behavior to us in a way that we understand. The one thing you should not do is to give up and abandon your dog. Somewhere a misunderstanding has occurred, but, with help and patient understanding on your part, you should be able to work out the majority of bothersome behaviors.

AGGRESSION

This is a problem that concerns all responsible dog owners, even breeds like the Cesky, who are known to be non-aggressive. Ceskies even get along with other dogs, a trait not often seen in terrier breeds. "Aggression" is a word that is often misunderstood and is sometimes even used to describe what is actually normal canine behavior. For example, it's normal for puppies to growl when playing tug-of-war. It's "puppy talk." There are different forms of dog aggression, but all are degrees of dominance, indicating that the dog, not his master, is (or thinks he is) in control. When the dog feels that he (or his control of the situation) is threatened, he will respond. The extent of the aggressive behavior varies with individual dogs. It is not at all pleasant to see bared teeth or to hear your dog growl or snarl, but

The Cesky is a bright and alert dog, a generally non-aggressive terrier that is friendly with all types of people and other dogs.

these are signs of behavior that, if left uncorrected, can become extremely dangerous. A word of warning here: never challenge an aggressive dog. He is unpredictable and therefore unreliable to approach.

Nothing gets a "hello" from strangers on the street quicker than walking a puppy, but people should ask permission before petting your dog so you can tell him to sit in order to receive the admiring pats. If a hand comes down over the dog's head and he shrinks back, ask the person to bring their hand up, underneath the pup's chin. Now you're correcting strangers, too! But if you don't, it could make your dog afraid of strangers, which in turn can lead to fear-biting. Socialization prevents much aggression before it rears its ugly head.

The body language of an aggressive dog about to attack is clear. The dog will have a hard, steady stare. He will try to look as big as possible by standing stiff-legged, pushing out his chest, keeping his ears up and holding his tail up and steady. The hackles on his back will rise so that a ridge of hairs stands up. This posture may include the curled lip, snarl and/or growl, or he may be silent. He looks, and definitely is, very dangerous.

This dominant posture is seen in dogs that are territorially aggressive. Deliverymen are constant victims of serious bites from such dogs. Territorial aggression is the reason you should never, ever, try to train a puppy to be a watchdog. It can escalate into this type of aggressive behavior over which you will have no control. All forms of aggression must be taken seriously and dealt with immediately. If signs of aggressive behavior continue, or grow worse, or if you are at all unsure about how to deal with your dog's behavior, get the help of a professional.

Uncontrolled aggression, sometimes called "irritable aggression," is not something for the pet owner to try to solve. If you cannot solve your dog's dangerous behavior with professional help, and you (quite rightly) do not wish to keep a canine time-bomb in your home, you will have some important decisions to make. Aggressive dogs often cannot be rehomed successfully, as they are dangerous and unreliable in their

---

THE TOP-DOG TUG

When puppies play tug-of-war, the dominant pup wins. Children also play this kind of game but, for their own safety, must be prevented from ever engaging in this type of play with their dogs. Playing tug-of-war games can result in a dog's developing aggressive behavior. Don't be the cause of such behavior.

behavior. An aggressive dog should be dealt with only by someone who knows exactly the situation that he is getting into and has the experience, dedication and ideal living environment to attempt rehabilitating the dog, which often is not possible. In these cases, the dog ends up having to be humanely put down. Making a decision about euthanasia is not an easy undertaking for anyone, for any reason, but you cannot pass on to another home a dog that you know could cause harm.

A milder form of aggression is the dog's guarding anything that he perceives to be his—his food dish, his toys, his bed and/or his crate. This can be prevented if you take firm control from the start. The young puppy can and should be taught that his leader will share, but that certain rules apply. Guarding is mild aggression only in the beginning stages, and it will worsen and become dangerous if you let it.

Don't try to snatch anything away from your puppy. Bargain for the item in question so that you can positively reinforce him when he gives it up. Punishment only results in worsening any aggressive behavior.

Many dogs extend their guarding impulse toward items they've stolen. The dog figures, "If I have it, it's mine!" (Some ill-behaved kids have similar tendencies.) An angry confrontation will only increase the dog's aggression. (Have you ever watched a child have a tantrum?) Try a simple distraction first, such as tossing a toy or picking up his leash for a walk. If that doesn't work, the best way to handle the situation is with basic obedience. Show the dog a treat, followed by calm, almost slow-motion commands: "Come. Sit. Drop it. Good dog," and then hand over the cheese! That's one example of positive-reinforcement training.

Children can be bitten when they try to retrieve a stolen shoe or toy, so they need to know how to handle the dog or to let an adult do it. They may also be bitten as they run away from a dog, in either fear or play. The dog sees the child's running as reason for pursuit, and even a friendly young puppy will nip at the heels of a runaway. Teach the kids not to run away from a strange dog and when to stop overly exciting play with their own puppy.

GET A WHIFF OF HIM!

Dogs sniff each others' rears as their way of saying "hi" as well as to find out who the other dog is and how he's doing. That's normal behavior between canines, but it can, annoyingly, extend to people. The command for all unwanted sniffing is "Leave it!" Give the command in a no-nonsense voice and move on.

Does your Cesky seem to be forlorn in your absence? It can be hard to know if your dog suffers from separation anxiety, as the symptoms only occur when the dog is alone.

Fear biting is yet another aggressive behavior. A fear biter gives many warning signals. The dog leans away from the approaching person (sometimes hiding behind his owner) with his ears and tail down, but not in submission. He may even shiver. His hackles are raised, his lips curled. When the person steps into the dog's "flight zone" (a circle of 1 to 3 feet surrounding the dog), he attacks. Because of the fear factor, he performs a rapid attack-and-retreat. Because it is directed at a person, vets are often the victims of this form of aggression. It is frightening, but discovering and eliminating the cause of the fright will help overcome the dog's need to bite. Early socialization again plays a strong role in the prevention of this behavior. Again, if you can't cope with it, get the help of an expert. As a Cesky owner, it is hoped that you will not have to deal with aggression problems, but it never hurts to be informed.

SEPARATION ANXIETY

Any behaviorist will tell you that separation anxiety is the most common problem about which pet owners complain. It is also one of the easiest to prevent. Unfortunately, a behaviorist usually is not consulted until the dog is a stressed-out, neurotic mess. At that stage, it is indeed a problem that requires the help of a professional.

Training the puppy to the fact that people in the house come and go is essential in order to avoid this anxiety. Leaving the puppy in his crate or a confined area while family members go in and out, and stay out for longer and longer periods of time, is the basic way to desensitize the pup to the family's frequent departures. If you are at home most of every day, make it a point to go out for at least an hour or two whenever possible.

How you leave is vital to the dog's reaction. Your dog is no fool. He knows the difference between sweats and business suits, jeans and dresses. He sees you pat your pocket to check for your wallet, open your briefcase, check that you have your cell phone or pick up the car keys. He knows from the hurry of the kids in the morning that they're off to school until afternoon. Lipstick? Aftershave lotion? Lunch boxes? Every move you make registers in his sensory perception and memory. Your puppy knows more about your departures than the FBI. You can't get away with a thing!

Before you got dressed, you checked the dog's water bowl and his supply of sturdy, long-lasting toys, and turned the radio on low. You will leave him in what he considers his "safe" area, not with total freedom of the house. If you've invested in child safety gates, you can be reasonably sure that he'll remain in the designated area. Don't give him access to a window where he can watch you leave the house. If you're leaving for an hour or two, just put him into his crate with a safe toy.

Now comes the test! You are ready to walk out the door. Do not give your Cesky Terrier a big hug and a fond farewell. Do not drag out a long goodbye. Those are the very things that jump-start separation anxiety. Toss a biscuit into the dog's area, call out "So long, pooch" and close the door. You're gone. The chances are that the dog may bark a couple of times, or maybe whine once or twice, and then settle down to enjoy his biscuit and take a lovely nap, especially if you took him for a nice long walk after breakfast. As he grows up, the barks and whines will stop because it's an old routine, so why should he make the effort?

When you first brought home the puppy, the come-and-go routine should have been

intermittent and constant. He was put into his crate with a tiny treat. You left (silently) and returned in 3 minutes, then 5, then 10, then 15, then half an hour, until finally you could leave without a problem and be gone for 2 or 3 hours. If, at any time in the future, there's a "separation" problem, refresh his memory by going back to that basic training.

Now comes the next most important part—your return. Do not make a big production of coming home. "Hi, poochie" is as grand a greeting as he needs. When you've taken off your hat and coat, tossed your briefcase on the hall table and glanced at the mail, and the dog has settled down from the excitement of

Cesky Terriers enjoy being part of a pack. They love time spent with their owners and appreciate the companionship of canine friends, too.

The way to stop a teething puppy from chewing a path of destruction is to provide him with interesting, safe chew toys to keep him occupied and to direct his chewing energies into acceptable behavior.

and sometimes you may think it's what your dog does best! A pup starts chewing when his first set of teeth erupts and continues throughout the teething period. Chewing gives the pup relief from itchy gums and incoming teeth and, from that time on, he gets great satisfaction out of this normal, somewhat idle, canine activity. Providing safe chew toys is the best way to direct this behavior in an appropriate manner. Chew toys are available in all sizes, textures and flavors, but you must monitor the wear-and-tear inflicted on your pup's toys to be sure that the ones you've chosen are safe and remain in good condition.

Puppies cannot distinguish between a rawhide toy and a nice leather shoe or wallet. It's up to you to keep your possessions away from the dog and to keep your eye on the dog. There's a form of destruction caused by chewing

seeing you "in person" from his confined area, then go and give him a warm, friendly greeting. A potty trip is needed and a walk would be appreciated, since he's been such a good dog.

CHEWING

All puppies chew. All dogs chew. This is a fact of life for canines,

that is not the dog's fault. Let's say you allow him on the sofa. One day he takes a rawhide bone up on the sofa and, in the course of chewing on the bone, takes up a bit of fabric. He continues to chew. Disaster! Now you've learned the lesson: dogs with chew toys have to be either kept off furniture and carpets, carefully supervised or put into their confined areas for chew time.

The wooden legs of furniture are favorite objects for chewing. The first time, tell the dog "Leave it!" (or "No!") and offer him a chew toy as a substitute. But your clever dog may be hiding under the chair and doing some silent destruction, which you may not notice until it's too late. In this case, it's time to try one of the foul-tasting products, made specifically to prevent destructive chewing, that is sprayed on the objects of your dog's chewing attention. These products also work to keep the dog away from plants, trash, etc. It's even a good way to stop the dog from "mouthing" or chewing on your hands or the leg of your pants. (Be sure to wash your hands after the mouthing lesson!) A little spray goes a long way.

DIGGING

Digging is another natural and normal doggy behavior. Wild canines dig to bury whatever food they can save for later to eat. (And you thought *we* invented the

doggie bag!) Burying bones or toys is a primary cause to dig. Dogs also dig to get at interesting little underground creatures like moles and mice. In the summer, they dig to get down to cool earth. In winter, they dig to get beneath the cold surface to warmer earth.

The solution to the last two is easy. In the summer, provide a bed that's up off the ground and placed in a shaded area. In winter, the dog should either be indoors to sleep or given an adequate insulated doghouse outdoors. To understand how natural and normal this is you have only to consider the Nordic breeds of sled dog who, at the end of the run, routinely dig a bed for themselves in the snow. It's the nesting instinct. How often have you seen your dog go round and round in circles, pawing at his blanket or bedding before flopping down to sleep?

Domesticated dogs also dig to escape, and that's a lot more dangerous than it is destructive. A

Dogs are attracted to their owners' belongings because these items smell like their favorite people.

dog that digs under the fence is the one that is hit by a car or becomes lost. A good fence to protect a digger should be set 10 to 12 inches below ground level, and every fence needs to be routinely checked for even the smallest openings that can become possible escape routes.

Catching your dog in the act of digging is the easiest way to stop it, because your dog will make the "one-plus-one" connection, but digging is too often a solitary occupation, something the lonely dog does out of boredom. Catch your young puppy in the act and put a stop to it before you have a yard full of craters. It is more difficult to stop if your dog sees you gardening. If you can dig, why can't he? Because you say so, that's why! Remember that terriers are the excavation experts of the dog world. A dog's propensity to dig varies with each individual, but it's your Cesky's instinct to want to get his paws dirty.

A Cesky isn't likely to knock anyone over while jumping up, but it's up to owners to decide whether this behavior is endearing or irritating. This young lady is entertained by her Cesky's two-legged antics.

JUMPING UP

Jumping up is a device of enthusiastic, attention-seeking puppies, but adult dogs often like to jump up as well, usually as a form of canine greeting. This is a controversial issue. Some owners wouldn't have it any other way! They encourage their dogs, and the owners and dogs alike enjoy the friendly physical contact. Some owners think that it's cute when it comes from a puppy, but not from an adult.

Conversely, there are those who consider jumping up to be one of the worst kinds of bad manners to be found in a dog. Among this group inevitably are bound to be some of your best friends. There are two situations in which your dog should be restrained from any and all jumping up. One is around children, especially young children and those who are not at ease with dogs. The other is when you are entertaining guests. No one who comes dressed up for a party wants to be groped by your dog, no matter how friendly his intentions or how clean his paws.

The answer to this one is relatively simple. If the dog has already started to jump up, the first command is "Off," followed immediately by "Sit." The dog

must sit every time you are about to meet a friend on the street or when someone enters your home, be it child or adult. You may have to ask people to ignore the dog for a few minutes in order to let his urge for an enthusiastic greeting subside. If your dog is too exuberant and won't sit still, you'll have to work harder by first telling him "Off" and then issuing the down-stay command. This requires more work on your part, because the down is a submissive position and your dog is only trying to be super-friendly. A small treat is expected when training for this particular down.

If you have a real pet peeve about a dog's jumping up, then disallow it from the day your puppy comes home. Jumping up is a subliminally taught human-to-dog greeting. Dogs don't greet each other in this way. It begins because your puppy is close to the ground and he's easier to pet and cuddle if he reaches up and you bend over to meet him halfway. If you won't like it later, don't start it when he is young, but do give lots of praise and affection for a good sit.

BARKING

Fortunately, the Cesky is not an indiscriminate barker as some of the other terriers tend to be. Their vocalizations are usually reserved for warning or alarming their owners about something. However, telling a dog he must never bark is like telling a child not to speak! Consider how confusing it must be to your dog that you are using your voice (which is your form of barking) to teach him when to bark and when not to! That is precisely the reason not to "bark back" when the dog's barking is annoying you (or your neighbors). Try to understand the scenario from the dog's viewpoint. He barks. You bark. He barks again, you bark again. This "conversation" can go on forever!

The first time your adorable little puppy said "Yip" or "Yap, you were ecstatic. His first word! You smiled, you told him how smart he was—and you allowed him to do it. So there's that one-plus-one thing again, because he will understand by your happy reaction that "Mr. Alpha loves it when I talk." Ignore his barking in the beginning, and allow it, but don't encourage barking during play. Instead, use the "put a toy in it" method to tone it down. Add a very soft "Quiet" as you hand off the toy. If the barking continues, stand up straight, fold your arms and turn your back on the dog. If he barks, you won't play, and you should follow the same rule for all undesirable behavior during play.

Dogs bark in reaction to sounds and sights. Another dog's bark, a person passing by or even just rustling leaves can set off a barker. If someone coming up your driveway or to your door provokes a barking frenzy, use the saturation method to stop it. Have several friends come and go every three or four minutes over as long a period of time as they can spare (it could take a couple of hours). Attach about a foot of rope to the dog's collar and have very small treats handy. Each time a car pulls up or a person approaches, let the dog bark once (grab the rope if you need to physically restrain him), say "Okay, good dog," give him a treat and make him sit. "Okay" is the release command. It lets the dog know that he has alerted you and tells him that you are now in charge. That person leaves and the next arrives, and so on and so on until everyone—especially the dog—is bored and the barking has stopped. Don't forget to thank your friends. Your neighbors, by the way, may be more than willing to assist you in this parlor game if it means a quiet dog on the block!

Excessive barking outdoors is more difficult to keep in check because, when it happens, he is outside and you are probably inside. A few warning barks are fine, but use the same method to tell him when enough is enough. You will have to stay outside with him for that bit of training.

There is one more kind of vocalizing which is called "idiot barking" (from idiopathic, meaning of unknown cause). It is usually rhythmic or a timed series of barks. Put a stop to it immediately by calling the dog to come. This form of barking can drive neighbors crazy and commonly occurs when a dog is left outside at night or for long periods of time during the day. He is completely and thoroughly bored! A change of scenery may help, such as relocating him to a room indoors when he is used to being outside. A few new toys or different dog biscuits might be the solution. If he is left alone and no one can get home during the day, a noontime walk with a local dog-sitter would be the perfect solution.

FOOD-RELATED PROBLEMS
We're not talking about eating, diets or nutrition here, we're talking about bad habits. Face it. All dogs are beggars. Food is the motivation for everything we want our dogs to do and, when you combine that with their innate ability to "con" us in order to get their way, it's a wonder there aren't far more obese dogs in the world. Ceskies may be terriers, but they are "chow hounds" who love to eat and can't resist when it comes to food.

Who can resist the bleeding-heart look that says "I'm starving," or the paw that gently pats your knee and gives you a knowing look, or the whining "please" or even the total body language of a perfect sit beneath the cookie jar. No one who professes to love his dog can turn down the pleas of his clever canine's performances every time. One thing is for sure, though: definitely do not allow begging at the table. Family meals do not include your dog.

Control your dog's begging habit by making your dog work for his rewards. Ignore his begging when you can. Utilize the obedience commands you've taught your dog. Use "Off" for the pawing. A sit or even a long down will interrupt the whining. His reward in these situations is definitely not a treat! Casual verbal praise is enough. Be sure all members of the family follow the same rules. There is a different type of begging that does demand your immediate response and that is the appeal to be let (or taken) outside for a potty trip. Usually that is a quick paw or small whine to get your attention, followed by a race to the door. This type of begging needs your quick attention and approval. Of course, a really smart dog will soon figure out how to cut you off at the pass and direct you to that cookie jar on your way to the door! Some dogs are always one step ahead of us.

Stealing food is a problem only if you are not paying attention. A dog can't steal food that is not within his reach. Leaving your dog in the kitchen with the roast beef on the table is asking for trouble. Putting cheese

Don't trust that your Cesky's knowledge of right and wrong will prevail in the face of temptation, because all resolve will crumble when that temptation is a tasty one!

and crackers on the coffee table also requires a watchful eye to stop the thief in his tracks. The word to use (one word, remember, even if it's two words pronounced as one) is "Leave it!" Instead of preceding it with yet another "No," try using a guttural sound like "Aagh!" That sounds more like a warning growl to the dog and therefore has instant meaning.

Canine thieves are in their element when little kids are carrying cookies in their hands! Your dog will think he's been exceptionally clever if he causes a child to drop a cookie. Bonanza! The easiest solution is to keep dog and children separated at snack time. You must also be sure that the children understand that they must not tease the dog with food—his or theirs. Your dog does not mean to bite the kids, but when he snatches at a tidbit so near the level of his mouth, it can result in an unintended nip.

INDEX

My Cesky Terrier

PUT YOUR PUPPY'S FIRST PICTURE HERE

Dog's Name _____

Date _____ Photographer _____